More Rhodes Around Britain

More Rhodes
Around Britain

Gary Rhodes

Photographs by Anthony Blake

BBC Books

Acknowledgements

My thanks to: David, Margaret and Joseph Levin; Celia and Martin Warbrick from Kitchens of Knightsbridge; Alice Portnoy from Neff UK; Anthony Blake and Joy Skipper; Jacqueline Korn and Borra Garson; Nicky Copeland and Wendy Hobson; Clare Adkins; the *More Rhodes Around Britain* production team; my *sous-chefs*, Stuart Busby and Wayne Tapsfield, and everyone at The Greenhouse; and, of course, my wife, Jenny.

This book is published to accompany the television series entitled *More Rhodes Around Britain*, first broadcast in 1995.

Published by BBC Books, an imprint of BBC Worldwide Publishing.
BBC Worldwide Ltd, Woodlands, 80 Wood Lane,
London W12 0TT

First published 1995
Reprinted 1995 (six times), 1996 (twice)
First published in paperback 1996

© Gary Rhodes 1995

ISBN 0 563 37158 7 (hardback)
ISBN 0 563 38759 9 (paperback)

Tested and edited by Wendy Hobson
Designed by Isobel Gillan and Tim Higgins
Illustrations by Kate Simunek
Photographs © Anthony Blake
Styling by Anthony Blake and Joy Skipper
Food prepared by Gary Rhodes
Cutlery and crockery provided by Divertimenti and Villeroy and Boch

Set in Ehrhardt and Ellington
Printed and bound in Great Britain by Butler & Tanner Ltd, Frome and London
Colour separation by Radstock Reproductions Ltd, Midsomer Norton
Jacket printed by Lawrence Allen Ltd, Weston-super-Mare
Cover printed by Clays Ltd, St Ives plc

PRECEDING PAGES Gary preparing four of his favourite cod dishes (see pp.66–73).

Contents

Introduction

Food glorious food.
Hot sausage and mustard.
While we're in the mood
Cold jelly and custard.
Pease pudding and saveloys
'What next?' is the question ...

Wonderful lines from 'Food Glorious Food' from Lionel Bart's musical *Oliver!*, based on Charles Dickens' brilliant novel. It's a stunning musical, and what a wonderful question: What next?! Well, these lines sum up everything I feel about the most basic dishes. For me, all food can be glorious and that certainly includes sausages and mustard, or cold jelly and custard (you'll find my recipes for these in this book!).

This is the story this book wants to tell you – good food doesn't have to be played with or overdressed; all it needs is to be put together simply and well. And, like the musical, I hope you're going to be asking for more! And *More Rhodes Around Britain* will give you more dishes to enjoy, more styles to try and a lot more options and scope with your cooking.

Over the years I have been in this industry, I have seen and learnt many things, but one thing that never seems to change is that too many chefs stick to strict rules and regulations. They create dishes and record recipes with with no room for change or variation. Well that's not what I want, or what this book wants to give you. I want to give you a lot more 'roads' to choose from, and whichever one you follow is going to be up to you.

Cooks' attitudes and feelings about cooking styles change with experience. Almost all chefs started their careers at a catering college or culinary school. It's at these schools that we, hopefully, learn most of the basics about cooking. Then it's time to hit the industry – and the learning programme starts all over again. But it so often happens that as chefs get to know dishes, they write them down and hide them. Of course, years on a lot of these recipes are shared in all kinds of cookery books, but in so many of them, the rules are strict. This is the recipe and that's it!

The way I have written this book is designed to help break that pattern. I want you to read it very differently from other cookery books. The recipes here are all reliable favourites of mine, and I hope will become favourites of yours, too. But every recipe involves room for movement and improvement! You can follow them, you can change them, use them as guidelines, follow the alternatives – the point is, it is up to you. There's a wealth of options beyond the recipes themselves.

Let's try a 'for instance'. If you happen to be reading a recipe and think, 'that sounds tasty' but haven't got the time to start making, say, a fresh custard or fruit coulis, don't be put off. Just look at the alternative simple method – use ready-made custard mix with tinned fruits or ready-made preserves, add a dot of fresh cream and, 'hey presto', you have a delicious ice-cream mix. Then, if you are saying to yourself, 'But I don't have an ice-cream machine' that's still no problem – the recipe will give you an alternative churning method. So everything is flexible – ingredients and methods. And the results? Well, I wouldn't offer you anything but the best!

Of course, I'd love it if you are able to try out some of the traditional methods – it may even surprise you how straightforward they are – but I live in the real world. Not everyone has the time to spend in the kitchen, but they do want excellent food, and there is no reason to compromise there. So, knowing you can eat great food whichever road you choose, have the confidence to adapt and you'll feel excited about trying out these recipes.

My cooking styles have certainly changed over the past fifteen years, which is all part of the learning process. You eventually find the style that suits you, adapting and absorbing from experience and turning it all to your own style. Even though my methods of cooking are still changing, I feel they will always be predominately British-based.

Travelling around Britain has been a lot of fun and almost a culinary education trip. It's been great to meet so many different people who get really excited and are so enthusiastic about good, simple, British dishes. One of the beauties of talking to so many people about cooking is you find out what the public are looking for and what everybody expects and wants from the industry. Giving people tastes and textures that they have never experienced and a style that's new is a great feeling, but what excites me even more is cooking dishes which evoke half-remembered taste sensations.

I don't cook for the food guides any more. I cook for the people, giving them food they are going to enjoy and not being afraid of serving anything, providing I'm convinced it can be cooked and eaten at its very best. I would love to promote British cooking around the world and to answer all our critics, because I have confidence in the dishes and the cooking styles we have to offer. It's all about believing in the recipe, knowing when a new dish is right, not adding anything that needn't be there, understanding ingredients and tastes that will complement each other.

I've included several 'feature' dishes in this book. When first putting this book together, I wasn't quite sure of this structure, it almost seemed like an excuse for giving similar recipes. But after some thinking I said to myself, 'If you've got ideas, then share them'. The whole idea of the features is to give you a variety of recipes, some developed along a theme or style, so basically you'll find loads of steamed sponges, ice-creams, risottos, savoury tarts and more – are you hungry? I hope so.

From *Rhodes Around Britain* to *More Rhodes Around Britain* has given me lots of new experiences in the culinary world – from cooking and training with Manchester United, being serenaded over cod, chips and mushy peas by the Nolan Sisters, driving a bright yellow Lotus, and cooking on an oil rig, to mixing with ostriches, singing to pigs, meeting on lighthouses and even being Gary Glitter's 'Leader of the Gang' – and what's next?

Well, first have a go at some of these recipes. They'll excite you and you'll be the one saying to all your guests, 'Just look at that!'

GARY RHODES

Notes on the Recipes

The basics of cooking don't change. Obviously we all try to develop new recipes and some new methods, but for most stocks, sauces or pastries it's 'back to basics'. So you'll find that I've included a few classic recipes in this book that appeared in *Rhodes Around Britain*, Chicken Stock and Veal *Jus* for instance. There are also recommendations for some ready-made products which remain the same. These are the foundations. I can promise you that everything else we do will be excitingly different!

You may find these few pointers useful when you start cooking.

1 Follow one set of measurements only, do not mix metric and Imperial.
2 Eggs are size 2.
3 Wash fresh produce before preparation.
4 Spoon measurements are level.
5 A tablespoon is 15 ml; a teaspoon is 5 ml.
6 If you substitute dried for fresh herbs, use only half the amount specified.
7 Mixed herb tea bags are readily available and can be used as an alternative to bouquet garni.
8 Unless otherwise stated, 'season' or 'seasoning' simply means seasoning with salt and pepper.
9 For information on alternative recipes for Veal *Jus* and stocks, see page 226.
10 If shallots are not available, substitute with half the quantity of onions.
11 I recommend Bournville chocolate where recipes call for 'good quality plain chocolate'.

Soups, Starters *and* Main Courses!

Looking at the title could be a little unnerving! Starters mixed with main courses? – this could be a long chapter! Well, don't worry. The reason I put them together is that almost every dish here can either be a starter or a main course, depending on how you serve it, and how much you serve.

ABOVE *Griddled Scallops with Crispy Aubergines (see p.42)*.
LEFT *Grilled Tuna with Salsa Dressing (see p.34)*.

All the recipes have been developed to give everybody plenty of scope and movement – some have also 'mini-features' so they include more than one dish in the basic recipe. There's everything from vegetarian to risottos and meat dishes – so I hope there's something to suit everybody and every occasion. So whether it's a light lunch you need, a summer barbecue, a family tea, or special dinner party – there's something here for you.

And don't forget that I don't want you to stop with these recipes. All the recipes should be an inspiration and spark off stacks of ideas of your own. So if you want to make the leek and Parmesan risotto but add asparagus and strips of smoked salmon and even top with a poached egg, why not?

The majority of starters are fish-based, ranging from mackerel and salmon to scallops, cockles and smoked eel. Fish is one of the bonuses of island-living; we have such wonderful fish available to us. In fact, only the tuna and king prawns are not locally fished. I didn't go out of my way to give mainly fish starters, but I do think fish starters with meat main courses does suit the British way of eating.

Gazpacho

This is a wonderful summer soup that has so many variations. My version has plenty of flavours and textures (see pp.18–19). Gazpacho can be served chunky-style or can be blitzed in a liquidizer and served smooth. It is traditionally served with everything raw, but if you want to make a winter Gazpacho, then just cook the ingredients in the olive oil first, then add the tomatoes and the rest of the ingredients to give you a spicy tomato and sweet pepper soup. To make the soups totally vegetarian, simply replace the Tomato Coulis and Chicken Stock with tomato juice.

SERVES 4

450 g (1 lb) ripe plum or salad tomatoes
1 red pepper
2 green peppers
1 yellow pepper
1 cucumber, peeled and de-seeded
1 garlic clove
1 onion
2 teaspoons tomato purée
2 tablespoons red wine vinegar

75 ml (3 fl oz) olive oil
300 ml (10 fl oz) Tomato Coulis (see p.232)
300 ml (10 fl oz) Chicken Stock (see p.222)
Salt and freshly ground black pepper
6–8 fresh basil leaves
12–16 fresh tarragon leaves

Remove the eyes from the tomatoes, then plunge them into boiling water for 8–10 seconds. Transfer to cold water and slide off the skins. This is called blanching. Once the tomatoes have been blanched, halve and de-seed them. Remove the stalks and seeds from the peppers. The tomatoes, peppers, cucumber, garlic and onion can now be minced through a medium cutter, finely diced or blitzed in a liquidizer until almost puréed.

Mix together the tomato purée and red wine vinegar. Whisk the olive oil slowly into the purée. Now add three-quarters of the tomato coulis and chicken stock. Stir in the minced ingredients and check the seasoning with salt and pepper. Lightly cut the basil and tarragon leaves and add them to the soup.

The soup can be as thick or thin as you wish. If you want to make it thinner, then add the remaining tomato coulis and stock.

Variations

A slice of white bread can be blitzed with the vegetables to give a thicker texture.

The flavour of the soup can be made hotter and more spicy by adding a few drops of Tabasco or Worcestershire sauce or even both.

Green Lentil Soup

This soup is a good winter dish. I personally like to eat it any time of the year, but on a cold winter evening a large bowl of this soup served with plenty of crusty bread in front of the fire (are you getting hungry?) is absolutely delicious. I also like to add some smoked bacon to this soup to lift the flavour and almost make it a main course dish. It can, of course, be a vegetarian soup by simply omitting the bacon and replacing the chicken stock with vegetable stock.

SERVES 4

25 g (1 oz) unsalted butter
1 tablespoon olive or vegetable oil
2 large carrots, diced
2 onions, diced
2 celery sticks, diced
4 rashers smoked streaky bacon, cut into
    strips

175 g (6 oz) green dried lentils
900 ml–1.2 litres (1½–2 pints)
    Chicken Stock (see p.222) or
    Vegetable Stock (see p.223)
Salt and freshly ground black pepper
150 ml (5 fl oz) milk or double cream
    (optional)

Melt the butter with the oil. When the butter begins to bubble, add the diced vegetables and bacon and cook for 2–3 minutes without colouring. Add the lentils and continue to cook for a few minutes. Add 900 ml (1½ pints) of the stock and bring to a simmer. The soup can now cook slowly, just ticking over for 45–60 minutes.

The lentils must be cooked all the way through, becoming tender and thickening the soup. If the soup is a little too thick, add the remaining stock. This is now a lentil broth. To help the lentils become more evenly spread through the soup, blitz gently with a hand blender or in a liquidizer to give a thick broth consistency with the bacon and vegetables not totally broken. Alternatively, the soup can be totally blended to a purée, in which case you'll need to add a lot more stock. Season to taste.

To finish either of the soups, you can add the milk or double cream to give a slightly creamy texture.

Cream of Onion Soup

This is a very simple soup to make using just a few basic ingredients. It's delicious served with thick slices of toasted French stick, finished with melting Cheddar or Parmesan. I like to serve it with Parmesan croûtons. Make these by slicing the crusts off a loaf of bread – any type you like: white, wholemeal, olive or anything else – and cutting it into 1 cm (½ in) dice. Cook the bread in a roasting pan with just enough olive oil to cover the pan in a pre-heated oven at 200°C/400°F/gas 6. As the croûtons are heating they will become golden and crispy. Every 1–2 minutes, turn the bread croûtons over to give an all-round colour. Once the croûtons are totally golden and hot they can be sprinkled with finely grated Parmesan and mixed to give an overall cheesey taste.

SERVES 4

50 g (2 oz) unsalted butter
675 g (1½ lb) onions, diced
2–3 celery sticks, diced
1 small potato, diced (optional)
1 leek (white only), diced

1 small garlic clove, chopped
900 ml (1½ pints) Chicken Stock (see p.222) or Vegetable Stock (see p.223)
2 tablespoons double cream or milk (optional)

Melt the butter in a pan. When the butter begins to bubble, add all the vegetables and cook for 8–10 minutes over a medium heat without colouring. Add the stock and bring to a simmer. Continue to cook for 20–30 minutes. The soup can now be blitzed in a liquidizer until totally puréed, then pushed through a sieve. If the soup is very thick, thin it down with a little extra stock.

As an extra added, stir in the double cream or milk to help the consistency and make a good cream of onion soup.

Lobster Bisque

Lobster bisque is regarded as the king of all soups and I don't think I can or want to argue with that. It is so rich in flavour and texture that it is really worth every effort in making it. If you make this quantity, you can freeze what you don't need.

Like all recipes, other flavours can be used. Crab, prawns or shrimp will all give you a full flavour. I use the same recipe to make a crab bisque to go with Crab Risotto (see p.60).

This recipe also holds lots of little extras – saffron, brandy, fennel – which all help to make this a better soup but can be left out for a basic bisque.

MAKES about 2.25 litres (4 pints)

1 × 450 g (1 lb) lobster
1.75–2.25 litres (3–4 pints) Fish Stock
　(see p.221)
50–75 g (2–3 oz) unsalted butter
1 tablespoon olive oil
2 large carrots, diced
4 shallots or 2 large onions, diced
2 celery sticks, diced
1 leek, diced
1 fennel bulb, diced
1 garlic clove, crushed
A few fresh basil leaves

A few fresh tarragon leaves
A pinch of saffron
6 ripe tomatoes, quartered
50 ml (2 fl oz) brandy
½ bottle white wine
50 g (2 oz) long-grain rice
Salt and freshly ground black pepper
A pinch of cayenne pepper
150 ml (5 fl oz) single cream (optional)
A few drops of lemon juice or brandy
　(optional)

If you are using a live lobster, bring the fish stock to the boil and drop in the lobster. Cook for about 5–6 minutes, then remove from the heat. The best way now is to leave the lobster in the stock until completely cooled. This will help flavour the stock and keep the lobster meat moist. If you are going to remove the lobster from the stock immediately, cook for 6–8 minutes, remove the lobster from the pan, then allow it to cool slightly before breaking the shell. Make sure you keep the cooking liquor to use in the soup.

Break off the claws and crack them with the back of a heavy knife to remove the lobster meat. Split the body and tail through the middle lengthways and remove the tail meat. Reserve the meat to garnish the soup. The lobster shells are used to flavour the soup itself. I prefer to crack the lobsters down (with a rolling pin) in a large saucepan as finely as possible, making sure I get the maximum taste. It's also possible just to break the shells down without finely crushing them.

Melt the butter with the olive oil. Add the roughly chopped carrots, shallots or onions, celery, leek and fennel with the crushed garlic, basil and tarragon leaves. Add the pinch of saffron and the tomatoes and cook for a few minutes. Add the crushed lobster shells and cook for a further few minutes. Add the brandy and boil to reduce until almost dry. Add the white wine and continue to reduce. Add 1.75 litres (3 pints) of stock, bring to the simmer and continue to simmer for 20 minutes.

Add the rice and bring back to the simmer for 20–25 minutes. The rice should cook until overcooked to create a starch and thicken the soup. Check the soup for seasoning with salt, pepper and a pinch of cayenne pepper. The bisque can now be blitzed in a liquidizer, with the lobster shells, to cream the soup, then pushed through a fine sieve. You now have a good, rich lobster bisque. The soup should be reasonably thick, well coating the back of a spoon. If it's very thick, add some more stock until you have the right consistency.

Always when making soups taste for seasoning once finished. Add the cream, and a few drops of lemon juice or extra brandy will always lift the taste.

Variations

This recipe works well with crab and also prawns or shrimps. If you want to make a shrimp bisque, use either 450 g (1 lb) of good quality shrimps or 450 g (1 lb) of shrimp shells. The same applies to prawns.

If it's crab bisque you are making, just use the same preparation and cooking methods. Once the claws have been cracked and the meat removed, the flesh from the remaining two joints can be taken out with the back of a spoon. All the white meat should be kept to garnish the soup, and all the shell and brown meat can be broken and used for the soup. If you want to keep the brown meat, simply remove the central undershell and scrape out all of the inside.

OVERLEAF *Mussel Chowder in the foreground (see p.20),*
Gazpacho (see p.13) and
Gary making Cream of Onion Soup (see p.15).

Mussel Chowder

Chowder is an old dish that was (and still is) a complete meal made with mussels, onions, potatoes and pork all cooked together (see pp.18–19). It was originally made with cider or white wine but over the years milk and/or cream were added instead. This recipe has two stages: the first one tells you how to cook the mussels and the second is for the finished soup. Mussels, of course, can be bought already cooked. The vegetables and white wine are an optional extra which will give more flavour to the stock; you can just cook the mussels in the hot fish stock. If you are just using water, increase the quantity of mussels to 675 g (1½ lb).

SERVES 4

For the Mussels

1 carrot, roughly chopped
1 onion, roughly chopped
1 celery stick, roughly chopped
½ leek, roughly chopped
1 bay leaf
25 g (1 oz) unsalted butter

1 glass white wine
750 ml (1¼ pints) Fish Stock (see p.221)
  or water
450 g (1 lb) fresh mussels, washed and
  bearded

For the Chowder

50 g (2 oz) butter
4–6 rashers streaky bacon, cut into
  2.5 cm (1 in) pieces
2 large potatoes, cut into 2 cm (¾ in)
  dice
3–4 large onions, cut into 2 cm (¾ in)
  dice

2 celery sticks, cut into 2 cm (¾ in) dice
600 ml (1 pint) mussel stock, Fish Stock
  (see p.221) or water
300 ml (10 fl oz) hot milk
150 ml (5 fl oz) single cream
Salt and freshly ground black pepper

To cook the mussels, cook the vegetables with the bay leaf in a little butter without colour until just beginning to soften. Add the white wine and boil to reduce until almost dry. Add the stock and bring the liquor to the boil. Add the mussels to the boiling cooking liquor and cook for a few minutes until the shells open. Discard any that do not open. Drain off the mussels, reserving the strained cooking liquor.

Melt the butter in a hot pan and add the streaky bacon pieces immediately. The pan must be kept hot to fry the bacon, allowing it to become golden; this will bring out the flavour of the bacon. There may be some bacon residue sticking to the base of the pan. Don't worry about this; it will give a good flavour to the soup. Once the bacon is coloured, add the diced potatoes, onions and celery and cook, without colouring, for a few minutes, reducing the heat of the pan. Add the mussel or fish stock or water and bring to the simmer. Continue to simmer for about 20 minutes or until the potato is cooked but not breaking too much. The stock will have reduced a little, increasing the flavour. Add the hot milk and single cream and bring back to the simmer, checking the seasoning with salt and pepper. Add the mussels and warm for 1–2 minutes before serving.

Onion and Anchovy Pastry Pieces

These are lovely little appetizers: the strength of the anchovy contrasting with the rich sweetness of the onion on crisp puff pastry. To achieve the rich sweetness of the onions they must first be caramelized, a slow process but worth it.

SERVES 4

4–8 large onions, sliced	1 egg, beaten
1 tablespoon water	100 g (4 oz) tinned anchovy fillets,
Salt and freshly ground white pepper	drained
175 g (6 oz) Puff Pastry (see p.212)	Olive oil

Place the onions and water in a large pan and place over a very low heat and keep on a low heat for anything between 2 and 4 hours. This process allows all the natural juices and sugars from the onions to be released. Once the onions have really softened and broken down, the sugar content will slowly start to caramelize. The onions will start to change colour and are only ready at a deep golden stage. Season with salt and pepper.

Meanwhile, roll out the puff pastry very thinly and cut into 2.5 cm (1 in) wide strips. Rest it in the fridge for 30 minutes to prevent it from shrinking.

Pre-heat the oven to 220°C/425°F/gas 7 and grease a baking sheet.

Place the strips on the baking sheet and brush with beaten egg. Spoon some onions down the centre of the strips, leaving 3 mm (⅛ in) down each side. Lay the anchovy fillets head to tail down the centre of the onions. Bake in the pre-heated oven for 8–10 minutes until the pastry is golden and crispy. Sprinkle with olive oil and cut into 2.5 cm (1 in) squares. Serve at once.

Potato and Parsnip Crisps

We all like crisps with lots of different flavours (although some of them I'm not so sure about!), but you can't beat home-made salted crisps with no other tastes to spoil. If you're having a dinner party and want something to go with pre-dinner drinks, then have a go at these. The parsnip crisps are brilliant, just deep-fried slices of parsnip, as easy as that! They eat well dipped in Cranberry Sauce (see p.239).

SERVES 4

2 large potatoes, peeled	Oil for deep-frying
2–3 large parsnips, peeled	Salt

Pre-heat a deep-fat frying pan to 180°C/350°F.

Shape the potatoes into neat cylinders, then slice them very, very thinly. Dry the slices on a cloth and fry a handful at a time until crisp and golden all the way through. Lift out and shake off any excess oil, sprinkle with salt and serve. The crisps will stay fresh and crisp for a few hours, or longer if kept in a sealed container. Always make sure you eat them within 24 hours.

For the parsnips, just slice very thinly lengthways and cook as for the potato crisps until golden all the way through. Lightly salt and serve. The parsnip crisps eat well dipped in cranberry sauce!

Duck Rillettes

Duck rillette is almost like a home-made coarse pâté. You can make it with pork or goose, as well.

Other flavours can be added to the duck before cooking to help flavour the cooking fat which will be used to hold the duck together. Orange peel can be left in (as for canard à l'orange*), or a clove of garlic, a bay leaf and sprig of fresh thyme. It's also possible to add some chicken or duck stock to this recipe for a moister flavour.*

Duck Rillettes are best served with slices of thick, hot toast.

Serves 4

4 duck legs
2 teaspoons rock sea salt

900 g (2 lb) duck fat

To make the rillette, simply follow the recipe for Confit of Duck (see p.88), cooking for a minimum of 2 hours. The duck meat has to be very tender and on the point of being overcooked.

Once cooked and still warm, take the duck legs from the cooking fat and remove the skin. Take all the meat from the bone, then break down the duck flesh, pulling it apart with two forks so that the meat is shredded rather than making a purée. Once the duck is reasonably finely shredded, start to add some of the strained cooking fat. This will give the meat a coarse pâté texture. After 150 ml (5 fl oz) has been added, check the seasoning with salt and pepper; season generously as they will be served cold. The duck rillettes should be moist and rich to eat. More fat can be added to make the pâté even richer (300 ml (10 fl oz) would be the maximum for this quantity). Spoon the rillettes into individual ramekins or one larger bowl and set in the fridge.

Once set, spoon a little of the liquid fat on top of the moulds and allow to set. This will keep the rillettes fresh as long as they are chilled. I suggest, however, that you keep them no longer than a week. Because of the high fat content the pâté will set quite firm in the fridge so take out about an hour before eating to appreciate the full flavour.

Potted Salmon

This is a good summer dish which can be made and set in a serving dish and used as a starter or main course. Always be careful when cooking salmon as the fish is delicate. It needs very little cooking and should always be pink in the centre to keep it moist and succulent.

To make the clarified butter, simply melt 350 g (12 oz) of unsalted butter until it foams, then the foam dies. Don't allow it to brown. Remove from the heat and leave to stand until the milky residue sinks to the bottom. Strain off through muslin.

You can make the salmon pots a few days in advance, but always serve them at room temperature. This will allow the butter to become softer and a lot tastier.

SERVES 4

450 g (1 lb) salmon fillet
300 ml (10 fl oz) clarified butter (see p.235)
2 shallots, finely chopped
1 small garlic clove, crushed
½ teaspoon ground mace
½ teaspoon salt

Freshly ground white pepper
1 tablespoon chopped fresh parsley
1 tablespoon chopped fresh tarragon
A few salad leaves
1 lemon, cut into wedges
Warm toast to serve

Trim the salmon fillet and cut into 1 cm (½ in) cubes. Warm the clarified butter to simmering point and add the chopped shallots. Cook for a few minutes until the shallots have softened. Add the garlic, mace, salt and pepper. Carefully spoon the salmon into the butter and return to a *low* heat. The salmon can now only be stirred very carefully to avoid breaking. As soon as the salmon has a light opaque colour, after about 5–6 minutes, remove it from the heat and allow to cool. Add the chopped parsley and tarragon.

Spoon the salmon into individual 7.5 cm (3 in) serving moulds, making sure that the shallots and herbs are evenly distributed between the moulds. Top up with the remaining butter. You may find that you have some butter left. This can be used for cooking fish, or frozen until the next time. Cool and chill the moulds until set.

Remove from the fridge and allow to return to room temperature. Turn out the moulds on to plates and garnish with salad leaves and lemon. This dish also eats well with warm thick toast.

Mackerel Croquettes

These croquettes can be made with other fish: salmon, cod, prawns or shrimps. In this mackerel recipe, I've added one small fillet of smoked mackerel. This is not essential, but it does enhance the whole flavour of the fish without being overpowering.

Serves 4–6

4 mackerel fillets, skinned
2 shallots or 1 small onion, finely
   chopped
Salt and freshly ground white pepper
1 glass white wine
1 bunch of spring onions, chopped
1 smoked mackerel fillet
225–350 g (8–12 oz) Mashed Potatoes
   (see p.133), without milk, butter or
   cream

Cayenne pepper
2 tablespoons plain flour
1 egg, beaten
100 g (4 oz) breadcrumbs
25 g (1 oz) unsalted butter and cooking
   oil or oil for deep-frying
1 lemon or lime, cut into wedges
1 quantity Lemon Butter Sauce (see
   p.228)

Pre-heat the oven to 200°C/400°F/gas 6 and butter a roasting tray.

To remove the central bones from the mackerel fillets, cut either side of the bones straight through the fish. This will leave eight strips of mackerel. Sit the fish on the tray with the chopped shallots, and season with salt and pepper. Add the white wine and cook in the pre-heated oven for about 6–8 minutes; the mackerel should only be just cooked. Drain off any excess liquor into a small pan, bring to the boil and boil to reduce by at least half. When the liquor has reduced, add the chopped spring onions and cook for 30–60 seconds until only just beginning to soften.

Flake the smoked and cooked mackerel fillets and add the spring onion reduction. Fold in 225 g (8 oz) of the mashed potatoes which will be enough to bind. The texture can be loosened by adding more potato. Season with salt and cayenne pepper. Shape into balls or croquettes about 6 × 2 cm (2½ × ¾ in). Leave to chill in the fridge.

Dust the croquettes lightly in flour, then pass through beaten egg. Roll in breadcrumbs and re-shape gently, if necessary, with a palette knife. To shallow-fry, heat the butter and oil over a medium heat and fry for 2–3 minutes until golden on all sides. To deep-fry, heat the fat to 150°C/300°F and fry until golden. Serve with lemon or lime wedges and lemon butter sauce.

Variations

Soured cream flavoured with fresh lime juice, salt and pepper makes a tasty dip.

Fillet of Mackerel with Caramelized Onions and Sweet Peppers

In this recipe, the mackerel is 'cooked' in a sousing liquor made with white wine, white wine vinegar and water and flavoured with pickling spices, star anise and herbs. The combination of the sharp, soused taste and the sweetness of the onions and peppers works really well. I like to present this dish on very thin short pastry discs. This gives the dish another texture, almost like eating an open flan.

Serves 4

1 quantity Shortcrust Pastry (see p.211)	A few drops of balsamic vinegar
4 mackerel fillets, skinned and trimmed	2 teaspoons fresh chives, snipped
2 tablespoons Basic Vinaigrette (see p.241)	1 cm (½ in) long

For the Peppers and Onions

4 large onions, sliced	1 tablespoon olive oil
1 tablespoon water	Salt and freshly ground black pepper
1 large red pepper, cut into strips	

For the Sousing Liquor

2 teaspoons olive oil	1 star anise (optional)
½ onion, roughly chopped	2 teaspoons pickling spice
1 small carrot, roughly chopped	85 ml (3 fl oz) white wine
1 celery stick, roughly chopped	85 ml (3 fl oz) white wine vinegar
1 sprig of fresh thyme	450 ml (15 fl oz) water
1 sprig of fresh tarragon	A pinch of salt
1 bay leaf	Juice of ½ lemon

Pre-heat the oven to 190°C/375°F/gas 5.

Roll out the pastry very thinly, cut into 7.5–10 cm (3–4 in) discs and leave to rest in the fridge for 20 minutes. Bake in the pre-heated oven for about 10 minutes until cooked through and crisp.

To caramelize the onions, simply place them in a pan with a tablespoon of water and cook, uncovered, over a low heat for about 2 hours until all the natural juices and sugars from the onions begin to colour to a rich, golden brown. This can be done in advance.

Cook the red peppers in the olive oil for 2–3 minutes until softened. Add to the caramelized onions and season with salt and pepper.

Meanwhile, make the sousing liquor. Warm the olive oil and add the onion, carrot, celery, thyme, tarragon, bay leaf, star anise and pickling spice. Cook for a few minutes until the vegetables begin to soften. Add the white wine, wine vinegar and water with a pinch of salt and the lemon juice. Bring to the simmer and cook for 15–20 minutes. Strain.

Place the mackerel fillets in the warm sousing liquor and bring almost to the simmer. This will just warm them through, keeping the fish succulent and juicy.

Sweeten the dressing with a little balsamic vinegar and add the chives.

Spoon the warm onion and pepper mix on to the pastry discs and lay the mackerel fillets on top. Spoon the dressing over and around the mackerel.

Variations

If you haven't got enough time to make the caramelized onions, simply fry 2 or 3 sliced onions in butter until golden brown and almost burnt. This will give a more bittersweet taste that will become a lot sweeter when added to the red pepper.

Fillet of Mackerel with Caramelized Onions and Sweet Peppers.

Grilled Mackerel with Mussel Stew

You can leave out the first stage in cooking the mussel stew if you wish and simply cook the mussels in fish stock, but the pre-cooking does give a lot more flavour to the cooking liquor. Turn to p.30 to see the finished dish.

SERVES 4

4 mackerel fillets
25 g (1 oz) unsalted butter

Salt and freshly ground black pepper

For the Mussel Cooking Liquor

1 tablespoon unsalted butter
1 carrot, diced
1 onion, diced
1 celery stick, diced
1 bay leaf

1 sprig of fresh tarragon
300 ml (10 fl oz) dry white wine
600 ml (1 pint) Fish Stock (see p.221)
900 g (2 lb) fresh mussels, washed and
    bearded

For the Stew

2 tablespoons olive oil
100 g (4 oz) unsalted butter
2 large carrots, cut into 5 mm (¼ in) dice
2 onions, cut into 5 mm (¼ in) dice
3 celery sticks, cut into 5 mm (¼ in) dice
1 bouquet garni (a few fresh basil and
    tarragon leaves and 1 star anise tied
    in a muslin bag)

300 ml (10 fl oz) dry white wine
2 teaspoons Pesto Sauce (see p.235)
2 large tomatoes, skinned, seeded and
    diced
1 teaspoon chopped fresh parsley

Butter and season a baking tray.

Trim the mackerel fillets and remove all central bones. This can be done easily by cutting either side of the bones down to the skin but not cutting through. Pick from the head and pull out the central bones; they will come away from the skin in one piece. Place the fillets on the prepared tray skin-side up. Brush the skin with butter and season with salt and pepper, then place in the fridge.

To cook the mussel liquor, melt the butter in a pan and add the carrot, onion, celery, bay leaf and tarragon and cook gently, without colour, until softened. Add the white wine and boil until the liquid has almost evaporated. Add the stock and bring to a rapid simmer.

To clean the mussels, run under cold water and scrape until all grit and beard are removed. Discard any that are open and do not close when tapped sharply. Drain from the water and drop into the cooking liquor. Bring the liquid back to the boil, stirring frequently. As soon as the mussels begin to open, drain in a colander, reserving the stock. This should now be drained through a fine sieve. Pick the mussels from their shells and check that they are clean from all impurities. Discard any that have not opened.

Warm a pan and add the olive oil and 25 g (1 oz) of the butter. Add the diced vegetables with the bouquet garni. Cook without colouring until they begin to soften. Add the white wine and reduce until almost dry. Add enough of the mussel stock until the vegetables are covered; you may not need all of the stock so just add a little at a time. Bring to a simmer and cook until the vegetables are tender. This will take about 8–10 minutes.

Pre-heat the grill.

Cook the mackerel fillets under the pre-heated grill until the skin is crisp. The fish will only take between 4–6 minutes.

While the mackerel is cooking, whisk the remaining butter into the liquor and add some pesto sauce to taste, the diced tomatoes, chopped fresh parsley and, of course, the mussels. Warm through and spoon into large bowls, distributing the garnish equally. Sit the mackerel on top and serve.

ABOVE *Grilled Mackerel with Mussel Stew (see p.28).*

RIGHT *Seared Peppered Salmon (see p.32) and
Cucumber Pickle (see p.244).*

Seared Peppered Salmon

This dish has very few ingredients but the method and preparation give lots of texture and taste. It's like eating warm salmon gravad lax with a fiery bite from the pepper.

The salmon can just be sliced and eaten, but the raw black pepper is very strong. The purpose of the searing is to take away that rawness, create texture and give aroma and bite. I like to eat it with Cucumber Pickle (see p.244) – classic salmon and cucumber combination with a difference!

SERVES 4–6

450 g (1 lb) salmon fillet with skin
1 tablespoon finely ground black pepper
1 tablespoon salt
1 tablespoon caster sugar
Olive oil
Lemon or lime juice

Trim the salmon fillet and remove any bones. Along the fillet run several 'pin' bones; these can easily be removed with tweezers or small pliers. The black pepper must be finely ground. You can do this in a food processor or in a pepper mill. Shake the pepper through a sieve to leave you with a fine grind. Mix with the salt and sugar and sprinkle over the salmon so that it is covered in one layer of ground black pepper. Wrap the salmon in cling film and chill. The salmon will be 'cooked' by the salt and sugar mix. This curing process can take as little as 1–2 hours, but I like to make this in the morning for eating in the evening.

Remove the cling film and cut the salmon into 2–3 cm (¾–1¼ in) thick slices. Pre-heat a frying-pan and brush with olive oil. Make sure the pan is hot. Sit the salmon in the pan and sear for about 15–20 seconds on one side. Providing that the pan is hot, the salmon will be almost raw but just coloured, with very slightly burnt tinges burnt on the pepper. Serve the salmon as a starter with a squeeze of lemon or lime juice or try it sitting on the cucumber pickle.

Smoked Salmon and Asparagus with Poached Egg Hollandaise

Cold smoked salmon on warm toast with warm asparagus and a gently poached egg just breaking on top sounds delicious – and it is. Lots of traditional flavours working together. This dish can be even better. I like to top the poached egg with Hollandaise Sauce (see p.235). It eats beautifully and gives a good finish to the dish.

SERVES 4

12–16 medium asparagus spears	Horseradish sauce or cream
Salt	225 g (8 oz) sliced smoked salmon
25 g (1 oz) unsalted butter	4 poached eggs
4 thick slices wholemeal bread	1 quantity Hollandaise Sauce (see p.235)

The first job is to prepare and cook the asparagus. To be certain of them being tender, lightly peel them from half way down to the base of the spears and cut about 2.5 cm (1 in) off the root. The asparagus will now be deep green from the top, changing tones down to white.

Drop the asparagus into boiling salted water and keep on full heat for 2–3 minutes, then drain. The spears will still have a nice bite in them. If you are cooking the asparagus in advance, simply drop them into ice cold water to refresh them. To re-heat, just drop them back into hot water for 30–40 seconds, lift out, season with salt and pepper and brush with butter.

Toast the bread and spread with a thin layer of horseradish sauce or cream; the flavour works really well with smoked salmon. Cover the toast with the salmon and sit the asparagus tips on top. Sit the warm poached eggs on top and finish with hollandaise sauce.

Variations

Instead of the hollandaise, you can use some Basic Vinaigrette (see p.241) with snipped fresh chives and just spoon it over the egg.

Grilled Tuna with Salsa Dressing or Sauerkraut

As you can see in the title, there's already two options for the tuna in this recipe, both of which are excellent. This dish also eats well as a main course. The tuna is best cooked and served as a medium rare steak, still nice and pink in the centre, to help the taste and texture. The tuna can be grilled or pan-fried, and should be served warm with the cold salsa dressing (p.243) or with the warm sauerkraut (p.94 – half the recipe will be enough for 4–6 starter portions).

If fresh tuna is unavailable or hard to get hold of, then other fish can be used – salmon, red mullet, trout or more. Tinned tuna can also be used and broken down with a fork and then mixed with the salsa dressing, this eats very well with a salad or even just a sandwich filling. The sauerkraut will only really work with fresh tuna steaks. The sauerkraut version is best served warm on the plate topped with some salad leaves and then the tuna steak sat on top. A good basic dressing with chopped chives goes very well with this dish.

The salsa is best served just sat next to the tuna with some green leaves (see p.10).

SERVES 4–6

4 × 100–175 g (4–6 oz) tuna fillet steaks	Basic Vinaigrette (see p.241)
Olive oil	Salsa Dressing (see p.243)
Salt and freshly ground black pepper	OR
Green or mixed salad leaves	½ quantity Sauerkraut (see p.94)

To cook the tuna, lightly brush the fish with olive oil and season with salt and pepper. The fish can now either be grilled on a hot grill or barbecue or pan-fried in a hot frying-pan. If the thickness of the steaks is 1 cm (½ in) the fish will only take 1–2 minutes on each side before it is ready to serve.

Toss the salad leaves in a little vinaigrette and arrange on plates with the steak.

Now all you have to do is decide – salsa or sauerkraut!

Grilling the tuna steak.

Crab and Salmon Fritters

These are a wonderful savoury starter that can also be cooked for hot canapés. The crab and salmon go together very well but both could be substituted with chopped prawns and cod or lots of other combinations. Once cooked until golden and crispy, I like to serve them with a soured cream lemon or lime dip made by flavouring some soured cream with lemon or lime juice, salt and pepper. This recipe comes in two parts: the crab and salmon filling and the choux pastry to bind it.

SERVES 6–8

For the Pastry

150 ml (5 fl oz) water
50 g (2 oz) butter
100 g (4 oz) plain flour

2 eggs, beaten
A pinch of salt

For the Filling

225 g (8 oz) salmon fillet
Salt and freshly ground white pepper
1 glass white wine
15 g (½ oz) unsalted butter
2 teaspoons olive oil
1 green pepper, finely diced

1 red pepper, finely diced
½ bunch spring onions, finely diced
15 g (½ oz) root ginger, finely grated
225 g (8 oz) cooked white crab meat
1 teaspoon chopped fresh dill
Tabasco sauce

Pre-heat the oven to 200°C/400°F/gas 6 and grease and season a baking tray.

To make the pastry, bring the water and butter to the boil. Remove from the heat and add the flour. Return the pan to a moderate heat and cook, stirring vigorously, until the paste comes away from the sides of the pan. Leave to cool. Gradually beat the eggs into the dough with the salt, leaving you with a smooth choux pastry mix with a dropping consistency.

To cook the salmon, sit it in the baking tray and add the glass of white wine. Cover with foil and bake in the pre-heated oven for 10–15 minutes, depending on the thickness of the fish. To check the salmon, it should be just firming to the touch, cooked like a medium steak, still pink in the middle. Once cooked, allow to cool. Reserve any cooking liquor.

Melt the butter with the olive oil. When it begins to bubble, add the peppers, spring onions and ginger and cook for 1–2 minutes. Remove from the pan and allow to cool.

The crab meat can be bought cooked and prepared (it's also possible to buy it frozen). Break it down and checked through for any broken shell. Add the salmon, peppers and dill and season with salt, pepper and a few drops of Tabasco sauce. Bind together with the choux pastry.

Heat the deep-frying oil to 180°C/350°F. Spoon the fritter mix straight from the bowl into the fryer or on to a floured tray before cooking. This gives a rustic natural shape. Fry the fritters until golden brown and crispy. If they seem to be cooking too quickly, then turn the fryer down to 150°C/300°F.

Note

The fritters should be no bigger than a soup spoon size. This will ensure they cook evenly. For little tasters, the size of a teaspoon should be just right.

Crumbled Baked Sardine Fillets

This dish can only really be made with fresh sardines. Sardines are great for grilling whole on a barbecue or under the grill, but the small bones can often be too much hard work. So for this dish, ask your fishmonger to scale and fillet them for you. If they are from large sardines you will only need three or four fillets a portion as a starter. Some of the small bones within the fillets can be removed with a small knife or tweezers. Any remaining ones are quite edible as for tinned sardines. The 'crumbled' is a breadcrumb and fresh herb mix sprinkled on top and grilled. Once crumbled, the sardines can be served on a simple salad or just with a squeeze of lemon. The dressing is one I used in Rhodes Around Britain *in a skate recipe with potato, fennel and artichokes, but it goes equally well with this dish.*

SERVES 4

6–8 sardines, filleted
Mixed green salad leaves

Olive oil
A few drops of lemon juice

For the Crumble Topping

25 g (1 oz) unsalted butter
1 large shallot or ½ onion, finely
    chopped
4 slices white bread, crusts removed and
    crumbed

1 teaspoon chopped fresh parsley
½ teaspoon chopped fresh tarragon
½ teaspoon chopped fresh basil
Salt and freshly ground white pepper
Juice of ½ lemon

For the Anchovy Dip

6 tinned anchovy fillets, drained
1 egg
25 g (1 oz) capers
1 garlic clove, crushed
2.5 cm (1 in) root ginger, peeled and
    chopped
1 bunch of fresh basil leaves

Juice of 1 lemon
½ teaspoon chopped fresh thyme
A pinch of sugar
50 ml (2 fl oz) warm water
225 ml (7 ½ fl oz) olive oil
225 ml (7 ½ fl oz) groundnut oil

Pre-heat the grill and butter and season a tray.

To make the crumble topping, Melt the butter with the chopped shallot or onion and cook without colour for 1–2 minutes. Mix the breadcrumbs and chopped herbs and season with salt and pepper. Mix some of the shallot butter into the crumbs until a crumbly texture is formed; you may not need all the shallot mixture. Add a few drops of lemon juice to the mix.

Sit the sardine fillets skin-side up on the tray. Sprinkle the crumble crumbs on top of each fillet. Place the sardines under a hot grill. Once the crumbs have become golden brown and crispy the fillets will be cooked; it will take just a few minutes.

Meanwhile, to make the anchovy dip, place all the ingredients, except the oils, in a food processor and blitz to a paste. With the processor still running, slowly add the oil as you would for mayonnaise. Season the dressing with salt and pepper and push through a fine sieve. The dressing will have a mayonnaise sauce consistency with a hint of green from the basil and capers.

Toss the salad leaves in some olive oil with salt and pepper and a few drops of lemon juice.

Spoon the anchovy dip on to the plates, forming a circular pattern. Sit the salad leaves on the centre of the sauce and place the crumbled fillets on top of the lettuce. The dish is ready!

Grilled King Prawns with Warm Spicy Relish

This dish is great as a starter or main course. King prawns can be cooked loose or made into kebabs (about five prawns per portion as a main course, or three or four as a starter) and cook really well on the open grill or barbecue. That's the beauty of a dish like this: it has so many combinations and options. The prawns taste delicious with the spicy relish, or you can just serve them on their own, with a squeeze of lemon or with mayonnaise. Also, you don't have to use king prawns. Just ordinary fresh prawns (or even frozen!) will also eat really well with the warm relish. You can eat the whole lot cold, warm under the grill or toss in butter in a frying-pan. That's how simple and easy this dish can be.

This relish can be made several days in advance and kept chilled, then either served cold or simply re-heated. Oh, and by the way, the relish also eats well with other fish and also chicken, so have a go!

To save time, you can use a tin of chopped tomatoes for this recipe; it's never quite the same but it does work. You can simply drain off all liquid from the can and add the tomatoes to the mix, or you can boil the tomatoes to reduce all the excess liquid until thick and strong in flavour before adding this to the mixture.

SERVES 4–6

20 raw king prawns	Salt and freshly ground black pepper
Olive oil	

For the Relish

8 plum or salad tomatoes	2 fresh green chillies, very finely diced
1 tablespoon olive oil	1 teaspoon tomato purée
2 large red onions, finely chopped	2 teaspoons demerara sugar
1 garlic clove, crushed	1½ tablespoons malt vinegar
2 green peppers, seeded and finely diced	Salt

Pre-heat a grill or barbecue.

If the prawns are whole including heads, then firstly remove the heads, then pick the shell from the tails, leaving the base of tail intact. The prawns can be placed on wooden skewers or left loose. Brush the prawns with olive oil and season with salt and pepper. The prawns will take about 1½–2 minutes per side on a hot open grill or barbecue, under a domestic oven grill or in a frying-pan.

To make the relish, remove the eyes from the tomatoes, then blanch them in boiling water for 8–10 seconds, then refresh in cold water and remove the skins. Quarter the tomatoes and remove all the seeds and water. Dice the flesh into 5 mm (¼ in) dice.

Warm the olive oil in a pan and cook the chopped red onions over a low heat for a few minutes until they begin to soften. Add the garlic, peppers and chillies, increasing the heat to medium. Continue to cook for a few minutes. Add the tomatoes and tomato purée and cook for about 6–8 minutes. As the tomatoes cook, all excess water will be released, creating a tomato sauce effect. However, this may seem a little too thin, so either continue to cook until a thicker tomato base is achieved or, and I think this is better, simply drain off all juices through a sieve and simmer the liquor on the stove until it begins to thicken, then remix with the other ingredients. You will now have a tasty warm chilli relish. To finish it off and give a spicy effect, mix together the demerara sugar and malt vinegar and bring to the boil. This mix will only take a couple of minutes to boil and reduce in volume. The consistency should be like a thick syrup. Add this to the relish a little at a time, tasting until a sweet and sour flavour is achieved. Season with salt and pepper.

Variations

If you are using straightforward, small, frozen peeled prawns, then why not mix some cold spicy relish with mayonnaise and turn the whole dish into a spicy prawn cocktail!

Griddled Scallops with Crispy Aubergines

This dish shows another taste alternative with basic ingredients. The sweetness of the scallops mixed with an almost bitter/burnt flavour of the frying works really well with the tomato and olive taste. For a quick salad dressing, just mix a few drops of balsamic vinegar with some olive oil and season with salt and pepper. Alternatively, a good extra-virgin olive oil would be enough on its own. Turn to p.11 to see the finished dish.

SERVES 4

1 large aubergine
2–3 tablespoons plain flour
1 teaspoon cayenne pepper
Salt and freshly ground white pepper
Oil for deep-frying
1 quantity Tomato Relish (see p.234)

6–8 black olives, finely diced
Basic Vinaigrette (see p.241) or olive oil
25 g (1 oz) unsalted butter
12 large scallops, cleaned and trimmed
Mixed green salad leaves such as rocket,
    curly endive, baby spinach

Split the aubergine lengthways and slice across thinly. Mix the plain flour with the cayenne pepper and a pinch of salt. Sprinkle the flour over the aubergines and lightly dust off any excess. These can now be fried in hot fat until golden and crispy. Drain off any excess fat and sprinkle with salt. The aubergines can be cooked before cooking the scallops and will stay crispy and warm before finishing the dish.

Warm the tomato relish, then mix the chopped black olives with a little vinaigrette or olive oil.

Heat a frying-pan until very hot but not burning, add a few drops of olive oil and a little butter. Sit the scallops in the pan, in batches if necessary, keeping the pan hot. If the pan is not hot enough, the scallops will simply begin to stew in their own juices which will spoil their taste and texture. Once they have coloured golden brown on both sides, turn them out, season with salt and pepper and repeat the same process if you are cooking in batches. This will only take 2–3 minutes.

Season the salad leaves and toss with a little olive oil. Spoon the warm tomato relish into the centre of the plate, making a circular platform for the scallops. Spoon the black olive dressing around. Sit the scallops on to the relish and place the salad leaves in the centre. To finish the dish, simply arrange the fried aubergines on top.

*Spooning the black olives around the tomato relish
while the scallops cook on the griddle.*

Fried Cockle Salad

Eating deep-fried cockles is delicious. They get really crispy and tasty. Just be careful not to fry too many at once otherwise you'll almost have a popcorn situation. So it's best to use a deep-fat fryer, or certainly a large pan with a lid.

The crispy cockles eat very well with Salsa Dressing (see p.243), although it is best to make the relish looser with more olive oil and lime juice, making it into more of a dressing.

You can buy cooked cockles in most fishmongers and supermarkets. If you buy live cockles, wash them well, removing any grit, then drop them into a pan of boiling water. The cockles will start to open after 30 seconds. Once they are open, drain off the water and leave the cockles to cool. Pick the cockles from their shells and leave to drain on a cloth.

Use whichever salad leaves you prefer. There's plenty of choice from lollo rosso and oakleaf to curly endive, rocket or lambs' lettuce.

SERVES 4

1 quantity Salsa Dressing (see p.243)	175–225 g (6–8 oz) fresh cooked cockles
2–3 tablespoons olive oil	2–3 tablespoons milk
Juice of ½ lime	2–3 tablespoons self-raising flour
Salt and freshly ground white pepper	Mixed salad leaves
Oil for deep-frying	A few drops of olive oil

Loosen the salsa relish recipe with some more olive oil and a few drops of extra lime juice. Check the dressing for seasoning with salt and pepper.

To cook the cockles, pre-heat the fat fryer to 180°C/350°F. Coat the cockles in milk, then roll lightly through the flour, shaking off any excess. Fry the cockles in the pre-heated oil for 1–2 minutes until golden and crispy. Lift them from the fryer and sprinkle with salt.

Spoon the relish on to the plates and scatter over the crispy cockles. Mix the salad leaves with a few drops of olive oil and season with salt and pepper. Sit the leaves in a small pile in the centre of the plate. The leaves should be standing high with the dressing and cockles being visible all around the plate.

Sautéed Scallop and Fennel Salad

Scallops are available fresh from many fishmongers, or you may find some good quality scallops frozen.

SERVES 4

4 fennel bulbs
Juice of 1 lemon
1 star anise (optional)
900 ml (1½ pints) water
Salt and freshly ground white pepper
50–75 g (2–3oz) unsalted butter

1 tablespoon olive oil
12 scallops, trimmed and roes removed
Green salad leaves
Basic Vinaigrette (see p.241)
1 tablespoon snipped fresh chives

Top and tail the fennel. Using a small knife, remove the core from the base of each fennel. Add the lemon juice and star anise to the water with a pinch of salt and bring to the boil. Add the fennel, cover and simmer over a medium heat for 15–20 minutes until just tender.

Pour off half of the cooking liquor and boil it to reduce to about 150 ml (5 fl oz). This will increase the flavour of the fennel. Add the butter to the liquor and whisk vigorously to make a butter sauce. For an even lighter and smoother sauce, use an electric hand blender to finish. This sauce can be kept warm and re-heated and blitzed before serving.

Slice the fennel 5 mm (¼ in) thick lengthways. Heat a frying-pan and add a teaspoon of olive oil to the pan. Fry the fennel slices on both sides until golden brown. Season with salt and pepper.

To cook the scallops, heat a frying-pan with a few drops of olive oil and a knob of butter. It is very important to cook scallops in a hot pan. This will colour and seal them quickly. If the pan is only warm, the scallops will begin to poach in their own juices, creating a different texture and taste. Once coloured and seasoned on both sides, the scallops are ready; this should only take 2–3 minutes depending on size.

To serve the dish, lay the fennel slices on the centre of a warmed serving plate and sit the scallops on top. Mix the salad leaves with a little vinaigrette and sit them in the centre of the scallops. Add the chives to the sauce and spoon around the plate.

Warm Smoked Eel and Broad Bean Broth on Mashed Potatoes

Smoked eel has a wonderful flavour. It's really good to use in a stew or simply cold with a horseradish sauce. The combination of flavours in this dish can work well together either for a cold or hot dish. This is a tasty hot version.

SERVES 4

450–675 g (1–1½lb) smoked eel

For the Stock

1 onion, chopped	2 sprigs of fresh tarragon
1 leek, chopped	A few black peppercorns
2 celery sticks, chopped	25 g (1 oz) unsalted butter
1 bay leaf	300 ml (10 fl oz) white wine
50 g (2 oz) mushroom trimmings	900 ml (1½ pints) Fish Stock (see p.221)
(optional)	or water
1 sprig of fresh thyme	

To Finish

350 g (12 oz) Mashed Potatoes	100 g (4 oz) unsalted butter
(see p.133)	300 g (10 oz) broad beans, cooked and
1 tablespoon finely chopped shallots	shelled
Juice of 1½ lemons	1 tablespoon snipped fresh chives
Salt and freshly ground black pepper	

Fillet and skin the smoked eel, saving all the trimmings for the stock. Hopefully, your fishmonger will do this for you, but if not, simply cut off the head and position the knife against the top half of the central bone. Carefully cut along the bone, removing the fillet of fish. Turn the fish over and repeat the same process. Now the skin can be removed. Slide your finger or thumb under the skin at the head end and it should tear off all the way along. The fillets may need a little trimming down the sides to remove any excess skin. Turn the fillets on their back to show the centre. From the head end to half way down there will be some bones. Simply position the knife under these bones and cut away from the flesh. You now have two long, clean fillets of eel. Cut these into diagonal 2.5 cm (1 in) pieces and keep in the fridge.

To make the stock, place the chopped vegetables, herbs and peppercorns in a pan with the butter and cook without colour for 10 minutes. Add the chopped eel bones and trimmings and continue to cook for 5 minutes. Add the white wine and boil to reduce until almost dry. Add the stock or water. If you are using water ask your fishmonger to give you some fish bones to cook with the eel trimmings. Bring the stock to the simmer and cook for 20 minutes. Stain through a sieve. Re-boil the eel stock and reduce to 450–600 ml (15–20 fl oz) to increase the eel flavour.

Re-heat 300 ml (10 fl oz) of reduced eel stock. Warm the mashed potatoes, add the raw chopped shallot and juice of 1 lemon and season with salt and pepper. Add the butter to the eel stock and whisk into a light frothy broth; a hand blender can be used to help this. Add the broad beans and warm through. Drop the pieces of smoked eel into the liquor with the remaining lemon juice and the chives and continue to warm. Spoon or pipe the mashed potatoes into the centre of a bowl or plate and spoon over the eel and broad bean broth.

Fillets of Smoked Eel on a Warm Potato, Onion and Beetroot Salad

The potato, beetroot and onion salad eats very well with the smoked eel. This dressing also tastes good with the addition of 2 teaspoons of horseradish, but I'm keeping this fairly simple to make.

SERVES 4

1 smoked eel, filleted and skinned (see p.46)
225 g (8 oz) new potatoes, cooked
120–175 ml (4–6 fl oz) Basic Vinaigrette (see p.241)
100 g (4 oz) caramelized onion (see p.26)

225 g (8 oz) cooked beetroot
Salt and freshly ground black pepper
1 tablespoon chopped fresh parsley
Mixed salad leaves, such as rocket, pousses (baby spinach), curly endive

Cut the smoked eel into 5–7.5 cm (2–3 in) slices, allowing three or four slices per portion. While the new potatoes are still warm, leave the skin on and cut them in half. Add three-quarters of the dressing and the cooked onions and continue to warm in the pan. Add the beetroot, making sure that it's carefully mixed in and not colouring all the potatoes. Check for seasoning with salt and pepper. Add the chopped fresh parsley. Season the remaining dressing and add to the salad leaves. Divide the potato and beetroot salad between four plates. Sit the leaves on top of the salads and lay the smoked eel on top. Finish with the chopped fresh parsley dressing.

Smoked Eel and Broad Bean Salad

This is as simple as it sounds – very few ingredients but plenty of taste. It is a very basic salad that can take on so many more flavours. Sliced, cooked, peeled new potatoes can be warmed in the horseradish or mustard dressing and placed underneath the salad, and a hot poached egg can be popped on the top before finishing with the broad beans. Breaking the egg yolk over the smoked eel and salad and mixing it with warm new potatoes in a horseradish and mustard dressing – delicious!

SERVES 4

450 g (1 lb) smoked eel fillet, cut into 7.5 cm (3 in) strips
150 ml (5 fl oz) Basic Vinaigrette (see p.241)
Juice of ½ lemon
Salt and freshly ground black pepper

1 teaspoon horseradish sauce or grain mustard
275 g (10 oz) cooked and shelled broad beans
Mixed salad leaves

The smoked eel should be at room temperature. Mix 1 tablespoon of vinaigrette with a few drops of lemon juice and re-season with salt and pepper. This dressing will be used to flavour the salad leaves.

Warm the remaining dressing and flavour with the horseradish sauce or grain mustard. Both flavours work well with smoked eel. Add the broad beans to the dressing and warm through. Toss the salad leaves in the salad dressing with salt and pepper and arrange the leaves on plates. Sit the smoked eel fingers on top of the salad, slightly overlapping. Spoon the broad bean dressing over the eels and serve.

Note

Broad beans should be cooked in boiling, salted water until tender. This can take 6–12 minutes depending on the size of the bean. Refresh under iced water and shell. The beans will have a rich, deep green colour and can be kept in the fridge and used when required.

Chicken Wing Salad

If you have chicken wings left after preparing chicken breasts, this is a great way to use them. Barbecued chicken wings make a quick and easy snack, salad or lunch dish and are very moreish.

Serves 4

900 g (2 lb) chicken wings	2 tablespoons soy sauce
1 tablespoon paprika	Olive or cooking oil
Juice of 1–2 lemons	Mixed salad leaves

Dust the chicken wings lightly with paprika. Add the lemon juice and soy sauce and toss together well. You can cook the wings now, but I prefer to leave them to take on the taste for anything from a few hours to a few days.

Lift the wings from the marinade. The best way to cook the wings is on an open barbecue. If you cannot do this, pre-heat the oven to 220°C/425°F/gas 7. Pre-heat a roasting tin on top of the stove with a little olive or cooking oil. Fry the wings until well coloured (even with a few burnt tinges), then transfer to the oven for 10–15 minutes.

Once the wings are cooked, pour over the marinade and bring to the boil. Remove from the heat and stir well. This will give the wings a paprika, lemon and soy glaze. Serve the wings on top of a mixed salad as a starter or in a big bowl for everyone to help themselves.

Variations

The wings also eat well with soured cream as a dip.

Spicy chicken wings for the Chicken Wing Salad.

Niçoise Salad

This country-style salad starter has over the years almost become a chefs' 'designer salad'. The tomatoes are laid at 12 o'clock, 3 o'clock, 6 o'clock and 9 o'clock and all the other flavours follow suit at 10 minutes to and 10 minutes past! Chefs could argue all day over what should be included. Should there be tuna or anchovies or both?

Well, I'm going to give you my version, with the first five ingredients coming from the original recipe and the rest the optional extras. I include tuna fish, but it's going to be grilled fresh tuna fillet to sit on top of the finished salad. Of course this can be left out of the recipe completely or replaced with broken tuna fish tossed into the salad.

SERVES 4

12 very thin slices French bread
4 tablespoons olive oil or garlic butter
1 head of soft lettuce or mixed salad
    leaves
8 black olives, stoned and quartered
2 plum tomatoes, seeded and cut into
    6–8 wedges

1 teaspoon small capers
100 g (4 oz) fine beans, crisply cooked
4–8 tinned or marinated anchovy fillets
8 new potatoes, cooked and sliced
Salt and freshly ground black pepper
4 × 100 g (4 oz) tuna fillet steaks

For the Dressing

6–8 tablespoons olive oil
2 tablespoons tarragon vinegar
½ teaspoon Dijon mustard
Milled black peppercorns
A pinch of salt

½ small garlic clove, finely crushed
½ teaspoon snipped fresh chives
½ teaspoon chopped fresh tarragon
2 hard-boiled eggs, roughly chopped

To make the dressing, simply mix all the ingredients except the herbs and egg in a jar or bottle, only adding the fresh herbs just before finishing the salad. If the herbs are added too early the tarragon vinegar will discolour them.

Brush the bread with olive oil or garlic butter. Toast until golden and crisp on both sides. Separate the salad leaves and add the olives, tomatoes, capers, fine beans and anchovy fillets. Add the potato slices and season with salt and pepper.

Season the tuna with salt and pepper and start to grill or shallow-fry for about 1–1½ minutes on each side, keeping the tuna medium rare to medium.

While the tuna fish is cooking, mix the salad dressing with the chopped herbs and chopped hard-boiled egg. Pour some over the salad and toss together with the toasts. Divide between plates and sit the tuna on top.

Raw Fennel Salad

Fennel is a vegetable that is not used enough. It has the most wonderful aniseed flavour and can be eaten raw or cooked. To eat raw fennel, slice it very thinly otherwise it will be tough. All it needs then is a good marinade or dressing in which it should be served chilled. Eating a good, cold fennel salad with dressing is so refreshing and works all your taste buds. This can be eaten as a side dish to go with fish, or on its own.

Cooked fennel has many uses in salads, fish and meat dishes, or as a vegetable. It can also be served just with a dressing or grilled or shallow-fried with sauces and spices. I like it with hot Griddled Scallops (see p.42), Seared Peppered Salmon (see p.32) or grilled fresh tuna cooked on a barbecue or hot grill.

SERVES 4

2 fennel bulbs	Juice of 2 lemons
7 tablespoons olive oil	Salt and freshly ground white pepper

Trim the root and tops of the fennel and slice on a machine or cut very thinly with a sharp knife into rings. Mix together the olive oil and lemon juice and season with salt and pepper. Add to the fennel rings. The fennel will now taste crunchy with an acidic taste of lemon and rich olive oil.

Variations

It's also nice to turn this recipe into a full starter served with a tarragon mayonnaise. Just add chopped fresh tarragon and a few drops of tarragon vinegar to Mayonnaise (see p.242). Spoon the sauce into a bowl and sit some salad leaves on top, finishing with the fennel.

Caesar Salad

This salad was a great invention. Caesar Cardini, from Caesar's Palace in Los Angeles, found himself with some unexpected dinner guests and quickly came up with this dish. I'm not sure if this is the absolute original. I think plenty has been added and taken away, but it always stays similar and very tasty.

You'll notice that the egg should only be boiled for 1½ minutes. This helps the binding of the dressing without the whites being totally raw. If you are still worried about this, then simply use the yolk from one or two hard-boiled eggs; the dressing will still work. Tabasco sauce is very hot and strong, so a dash must literally be just one or two drops. Marinated anchovy fillets are bought soaked in a vinegar liquor, making them packed with flavour and taste.

SERVES 4

For the Salad

6 little gem or 2 cos lettuces

12 marinated or 8 tinned anchovy fillets

4 thick slices wholemeal bread

Olive oil

25 g (1 oz) Parmesan, grated

50 g (2 oz) Parmesan flakes

For the Dressing

15 g (½ oz) anchovy fillets, drained and chopped

2 teaspoons capers

2 teaspoons Worcestershire sauce

½ teaspoon Dijon mustard

A dash of Tabasco sauce

Juice of ½ lemon

½ garlic clove, crushed

2 tablespoons finely grated Parmesan

1 egg, boiled for 1½ minutes only

150–300 ml (5–10 fl oz) extra-virgin olive oil

Freshly ground black pepper

Break down the lettuces into separate leaves. Split the anchovy fillets into strips. Remove the crusts off the bread and cut into 1 cm (½ in) squares. These can be shallow-fried, toasted or (and this is what I do!) sprinkled with olive oil and baked in a pre-heated oven at 200°C/400°F/gas 6. Keep turning them every minute or so until golden brown and crunchy. Cooking them this way prevents them from becoming soaked in oil. While still hot, toss them in the grated Parmesan.

The quickest way to make the dressing is to place all the ingredients into a blender, using just 150 ml (5 fl oz) of oil to start with, and blitz until thick and creamy. Check for seasoning. Be careful of using any salt in this dressing because of the high salt content of the anchovies. The dressing can be pushed through a sieve or left rustic, which will give you more texture. If necessary, you can add a little more oil at a time. The consistency should be thick and emulsified, coating the back of a spoon.

To assemble the salad, toss the lettuce leaves in the dressing, making sure they are all coated. Add the anchovies, croûtons and half of the Parmesan flakes and divide between the salad bowls. Sprinkle with the remaining Parmesan and serve.

Caesar Salad.

Risotto

Risotto is a speciality rice dish from northern Italy and there is no other rice dish quite like it. The best rice all round to use (and the only one for this dish really) is arborio. This is an almost round rice that has an outer layer that creates a wonderful creamy texture as it cooks. It's the cooking method that creates this consistency: just adding a little hot stock at a time which, as it's braising on top of the stove, starts to break down the layers.

Risotto can be as basic and easy or as exciting and difficult as you wish. Probably the classic Italian risotto is Milanese, which is made with saffron and Parmesan; quite a simple dish that sparked off many variations.

All my risotto recipes are flexible; you can change the ingredients to suit yourself. One ingredient that is used in many Italian risottos is beef bone marrow. Added to the onions while they are softening in the butter and olive oil, this adds a richness to the dish which lifts the flavour and texture. It can be used in any of these risottos just adding 25–50 g (1–2 oz) per recipe. Risottos can also be lovely vegetarian dishes providing vegetable stock is used.

Here are the basic quantities for any risotto – the proportions of rice, stock, onions and butter are the same – a simple blueprint for making up your own.

225 g (8 oz) arborio rice

1.2 litres (2 pints) Vegetable Stock (see p.223), Chicken Stock (see p.222) or Fish Stock (see p.221)

100–175 g (4–6 oz) unsalted butter

2 onions, finely chopped

Finely grated Parmesan added at the end of cooking enriches all the flavours and makes the consistency even more creamy.

Mushroom Risotto with Crispy Black Pudding

Mushrooms and black pudding are a traditional British combination, usually served at breakfast. They work together very well in this recipe, contrasting the creaminess of the risotto with the crispy, rich black pudding. The best mushrooms to use in this recipe are the open cup or flat. These have an almost meaty texture and a much better flavour.

SERVES 4–8

100–175 g (4–6 oz) unsalted butter
1 tablespoon olive oil
2 onions, finely chopped
25–50 g (1–2 oz) bone marrow, chopped (optional)
1.2 litres (2 pints) Vegetable Stock (see p.223) or Chicken Stock (see p.222)
225–350 g (8–12 oz) open cup or flat mushrooms, sliced

225 g (8 oz) arborio rice
1 black pudding, cut into 1 cm (½ in) dice
1–2 tablespoons freshly grated Parmesan
Salt and freshly ground black pepper
Parmesan flakes

Melt the butter with the olive oil in a large pan. Add the chopped onions and chopped bone marrow, if using, and cook without colouring for 2–3 minutes. Meanwhile, bring the stock to the boil. Add the sliced mushrooms to the onions, increasing the heat of the pan. Allow the mushrooms to cook for 2–3 minutes. Add the rice and continue to cook over a medium heat for a further minute. Add the hot stock a ladle at a time, allowing it to become absorbed in the rice and evaporate before adding another ladle. Continue this process, stirring almost continuously to keep an even cooking. This will take 20–30 minutes. When the risotto is almost cooked, the black pudding can be either pan-fried until crispy or cooked under the grill.

Once the risotto is cooked, add some grated Parmesan and check the consistency is of a rich creamy texture. Season with salt and pepper and spoon on to a plate or into bowls. Sprinkle with Parmesan flakes, crispy black pudding and a few drops of olive oil.

ABOVE *Crab Risotto (see p.60).*

OPPOSITE *Checking the flavour of the risotto.*

Crab Risotto

Seafood risottos are really delightful to eat. In Italy, meat or fish are almost always included in the dish rather than served with it, making the risotto a complete meal in itself (see p.58).

For the maximum crab flavour, it's best to use fresh crab cooked in fish stock. This will leave you with a good crab stock to lift the flavour. If you are using fresh crab, follow the cooking method from the bisque recipe on p.16. Otherwise cooked white crab meat can be obtained from most fishmongers or supermarkets, either fresh or frozen.

I also like to serve the risotto finished with a border of crab bisque (see Lobster Bisque p.16). This is well worth the effort; it totally lifts the whole dish. But remember that tinned crab bisque is available – one or two tablespoons will be enough.

SERVES 4–6

1.2 litres (2 pints) Fish Stock (see p.221)
100–175 g (4–6 oz) unsalted butter
1 tablespoon olive oil
2 onions, finely chopped
25-50 g (1–2 oz) bone marrow, chopped
(optional)
225 g (8 oz) arborio rice

225 g (8 oz) white crab meat, shredded
Salt and freshly ground white pepper
1–2 tablespoons finely grated Parmesan
(optional)
Crab Bisque (see p.16) or tinned (optional)
Parmesan flakes (optional)
Olive oil

Bring the fish or crab stock to the simmer. Melt 100 g (4 oz) of the butter with the olive oil, add the onions and cook for 3–4 minutes without colouring. As the onions begin to soften, add the bone marrow, if using. Add the rice and cook for 2–3 minutes. Now add two ladles of hot stock, keeping the rice over a medium heat. The hot stock will create a steam and immediately begin to evaporate. Because you only add a ladle at a time, the rice will absorb the stock without becoming totally encased. This is the process that helps cream the risotto. Continue to add the stock a little at a time until the rice is tender; this will take about 20 minutes. The finished texture of the rice should have the slightest bite.

Add the crab meat and the remaining butter and season with salt and pepper. I also like to add a little Parmesan to lift the taste. The consistency should not be at all stodgy but rich and creamy. Some crab bisque can be added to the finished risotto to improve the flavour and consistency even more; use a few spoonfuls.

The risotto is now ready to serve. If you are using crab bisque, spoon the risotto into bowls and pour some more bisque around. The risotto can also be garnished with Parmesan flakes and a trickle of olive oil.

Variations

This recipe can be used for lobster, prawn or shrimp risotto. Mussels also make a good risotto. Cook them first in fish stock, then use the resulting mussel stock for the risotto. Don't add the cooked mussels to the rice until the end otherwise they will be overcooked and tough.

Leek and Parmesan Risotto with a Warm Poached Egg

The traditional way to poach an egg is to bring a deep pan of water to a rolling boil. Add a generous quantity of wine or malt vinegar, then crack the egg into the water. Poach for about 3 minutes until the white has set. Remove from the pan and place in a bowl of cold water to stop the cooking or serve immediately.

Serves 4

1.2 litres (2 pints) Vegetable Stock (see p.223) or Chicken Stock (see p.222)
450 g (1 lb) leeks, trimmed and sliced
175 g (6 oz) unsalted butter
2 onions, finely chopped
1 small garlic clove, crushed
225 g (8 oz) arborio rice
3–4 tablespoons grated Parmesan
Salt and freshly ground white pepper
4 poached eggs
2–3 tablespoons Basic Vinaigrette (see p.241) or seasoned olive oil
1 tablespoon snipped fresh chives
Fresh Parmesan flakes (optional)

Bring the stock to the boil and add the sliced leeks. Bring back to the boil and drain the leeks off, reserving the leeks and stock separately. Melt the butter in a large pan, add the onions and garlic and cook for a few minutes without colouring until softened. Add the rice and cook for a further minute. Start to add the hot stock a ladle at a time and cook over a medium heat, allowing the rice to absorb almost all the stock before adding more stock. Continue to add, cook and stir until the rice is softening but not getting to a purée creamed stage; this will take about 20 minutes.

Stir in the Parmesan. The more you add, the richer the taste will become. The Parmesan will also thicken the risotto so add more stock to give a loose consistency if necessary. Add the leeks, season with salt and pepper and warm through. Spoon into the bowls and sit a warm poached egg on top. Mix the dressing or olive oil with the chives and spoon a little over the eggs. Sprinkle with some Parmesan flakes to finish.

Main
Courses

Well, here we are, the course that we balance our menus around. That's really the best way of building a dinner party or restaurant menu. You first look at the main course and whichever one you choose will help determine your starter and pudding.

ABOVE *Roast Parsnip and Chestnut Crumble on Bubble and Squeak (see p.118).*
LEFT *Home-made Pork Pie (see p.92).*

I must admit if I'm cooking for myself and maybe a few friends I don't worry too much about balancing all the dishes; I tend just to cook what I feel like eating. However, balancing dishes is very important. Making sure that all the dishes aren't coated with cream sauces or too rich, for example, will give you a healthier and tastier meal.

The chapter has been broken down into smaller sections: Fish, Meat and Poultry, Vegetarian Dishes and Vegetables. Amongst these there are some more features of savoury crumbles and tarts to keep you busy!

Fish

I've kept this part of the chapter relatively short, because the majority of dishes in the Starters section are fish, all of which are suitable to serve as main courses as well.

Cooking with fish is so enjoyable, the first advantage being the variety available, all with their different textures, colours and flavours. The texture of the fish will also determine how it should be cooked: pan-fried, deep-fried, grilled, braised or stewed.

One of my favourite fish is cod (you can probably tell, I've featured four cod dishes in this chapter!). A fresh, thick cod fillet is built up of large white flakes, and when simply grilled or pan-fried with just a knob of butter and kept moist, the centre of the flakes become almost transparent and juicy.

When I ask for fillets, I do mean fillets. Your fishmonger should be able to help you out with this. A lot of cod, for instance, is sold as steaks cut straight through the bone. It looks very nice but can be difficult to handle when eating. On top of that, cutting straight through will break down the texture of the fish, loosing those lovely large flakes.

Skate is different altogether. This is normally sold on the bone and as skate wings. When cooking a skate wing dish, it's usually pan-fried and finished with nut brown butter, capers and parsley. Well in one or two of these skate dishes I'm using fillets. These are quite easy to cut away from the bone and when pan-fried golden brown and crispy can become part of a whole dish a lot easier to eat. Sitting the fillet on top of salads or pasta works really well and you certainly can't do that if it's a straight skate wing!

All the fish dishes in this chapter can be adapted to the fish you want to use. So instead of cod or skate, why not try the recipe with turbot, brill, halibut, salmon or even something else.

Roast Cod on Potatoes with Fried Anchovies

This has to be my favourite fish dish in the book (see pp.70–71) As with most of the recipes, another fish can be used or you can leave the fish out and serve the dish as a warm potato salad with crispy anchovies. Marinated anchovies are sold loosely, not in tins.

Because I'm roasting this cod, I want to keep the skin on. When shallow-fried then roasted, cod skin comes up very crisp and tasty; it's good enough to eat on its own!

SERVES 4

450 g (1 lb) new potatoes
Salt and freshly ground white pepper
150 ml (5 fl oz) Vierge Dressing (see
    p.243) or olive oil
Juice of 1 lemon
25 g (1 oz) unsalted butter
2 teaspoons cooking oil
4 × 175–225 g (6–8 oz) cod fillets
12 marinated anchovies
1 teaspoon self-raising flour
¼ teaspoon cayenne

2–3 tablespoons milk
Oil for deep-frying
1 tablespoon fine or chopped capers
2 shallots or ½ onion, very finely
    chopped
½ teaspoon chopped fresh parsley
1 teaspoon chopped fresh coriander
1 teaspoon chopped fresh tarragon
1 teaspoon chopped fresh basil
A few green salad leaves (optional)

Pre-heat the oven to 200°C/400°F/gas 6.

Cook the new potatoes, then peel off the skin. Cut into 5 mm (¼ in) slices while still warm, then season with salt and pepper. Add 1–2 tablespoons of dressing or olive oil and the juice of ½ lemon. Season again with salt and pepper and keep warm.

Melt the butter and oil in a hot pan. Season the cod with salt and pepper and place in the pan skin-side down. Cook until deep in colour, then turn over and finish cooking in the oven for 5–8 minutes, depending on the thickness of the cod.

Split the anchovies through the centre. Mix the flour with the cayenne and a pinch of salt. Dip the anchovies in the milk, then roll in the cayenne flour. Deep-fry in hot oil until very crispy. If you don't have a deep-fat fryer, cook them in about 5 mm (¼ in) of hot oil in a frying-pan, but don't let it get so hot so that it smokes, and keep turning the fish in the pan until they are crispy.

To finish the dish, warm the remaining dressing or oil and add the capers and shallots or onion with a squeeze of lemon juice and the herbs. Season with salt and pepper. The dressing should be served warm.

Spoon some potatoes on to plates and top with a few green salad leaves. Spoon the dressing all around and sit a few fried anchovy fillets on top of the dressing. Finish the dish with the roasted cod fillet on top with the crispy skin-side showing. Brush with a little butter to finish.

Fried Anchovies.

Pan-fried Cod on Fennel and Potato Salad with Tartare Dressing

Cod, chips and tartare sauce is probably Britain's most famous and classic fish dish, and cooked well with a good, crispy batter and a tartare made with fresh mayonnaise, you can't beat it (see overleaf). I decided to use nearly all of those tastes in this dish: the fresh cod, potatoes and tartare sauce flavour without the mayonnaise. To this I've added some fresh fennel which, with its slight aniseed flavour, really helps the potatoes and fish. You can, of course, leave out the fennel and I promise you'll still enjoy this lighter version of our old favourite.

SERVES 4

4 × 175–225 g (6–8 oz) cod fillets	50 g (2 oz) unsalted butter
2 tablespoons plain flour	1 tablespoon olive oil

For the Dressing

2 teaspoons capers	½ bunch of fresh parsley
2 teaspoons chopped cocktail gherkins	1–2 tablespoons olive oil
2 teaspoons chopped shallot or onion	Salt and freshly ground black pepper

For the Fennel and Potatoes

2 large fennel bulbs	50 ml (2 fl oz) Basic Vinaigrette
2 lemons	(see p.241)
275 g (10 oz) new potatoes	

To make the dressing, place the capers, gherkins and shallot or onion in a food processor and blitz until almost puréed. Add the parsley and 1 tablespoon of olive oil. Continue to blitz until the parsley is finely chopped. Season with salt and pepper. If the dressing is very thick, simply add more olive oil. This dressing keeps well for 24 hours in the fridge.

To cook the fennel, top and tail the bulbs and remove some of the core at the base. Bring about 1.2 litres (2 pints) of water to the boil (enough to cover the fennel) with the juice of 1 lemon and a pinch of salt. Place the fennel into the water and cover with a lid, bring back to the boil, then simmer until just tender; this will take 15–20 minutes. Leave to cool. Cut the fennel in half lengthways, then each half into 5–6 slices lengthways.

Meanwhile, boil the new potatoes until tender, then drain, peel off the skins and cut the potatoes in half. Mix the basic dressing with the juice of the remaining lemon and add to the new potatoes and fennel slices. Season with salt and pepper and bring up to the simmer.

To cook the cod, lightly flour and season each fillet and brush with butter on the skin side. Heat a frying-pan with a little olive oil. Lay the cod butter-side down into the pan and cook until golden brown. Turn the fish in the pan and continue to cook. The cod will take about 6–8 minutes to cook.

To serve, spoon the tartare dressing into bowls or plates and sit the fennel and potatoes on top. Finish by sitting the cod on to the garnish.

OVERLEAF *Clockwise, starting at the front:*
Deep-fried Cod in Batter (see p.72);
Pan-fried Cod on Pecorino Mashed Potatoes and Spinach (see p.73);
extra Fried Anchovies (see p.66);
Pan-fried Cod on Fennel and Potato Salad with Tartare Dressing (see p.68);
Roast Cod on Potatoes with Fried Anchovies (see p.66).

Deep-fried Cod in Batter

This must be the quickest batter to make. It's just lager and some salt and self-raising flour. The only secret is to make sure the batter is very thick, almost too thick. As the cod is cooking, the batter will soufflé, keeping it light and crisp (see preceding pages). If the batter is too thin, it tends to stick to the fish and become heavy. You can use the same recipe for any deep-fried fish, sausages or whatever. It also eats well with Tomato Sauce (see p.233).

SERVES 4

450 g (1 lb) self-raising flour
Salt and freshly ground black pepper
4 × 175–225 g (6–8 oz) cod fillets,
   skinned and boned

600 ml (1 pint) lager
A pinch of salt
Oil for deep-frying

For the Tartare Sauce

300 ml (10 fl oz) Mayonnaise (see p.242)
25 g (1 oz) gherkins, chopped
25 g (1 oz) capers, chopped

25 g (1 oz) onion, finely chopped
2 teaspoons chopped fresh parsley
A squeeze of lemon juice

Season a spoonful of flour with salt and pepper. Lightly dust each fillet in the flour.

Whisk half the remaining flour into the lager with a pinch of salt, then gradually add the flour a spoonful at a time to make a thick batter. Dip the cod into the batter. Heat the oil to 180°C/350°F, then fry the cod until golden.

To make the sauce, mix all the ingredients together and season with lemon juice, salt and pepper. Serve with the crispy fried cod.

Pan-fried Cod on Pecorino Mashed Potatoes and Spinach

You don't have to stick to cod with this recipe: halibut, haddock, turbot or brill can all be used and taste just as good (see pp.70–71).

Pecorino is an Italian ewes' milk cheese with a similar texture to Parmesan. I like to use smoked Pecorino for extra taste. Pecorino cheeses were introduced to me by Giovanni, an Italian friend who lives in South Wales. Giovanni makes his own 'Pecorinos' with Welsh ewes' milk – and it works! The cheese is lovely. If you have trouble finding Pecorino, just use Parmesan.

All I do with this recipe is add grated smoked Pecorino to hot mashed potatoes to give you a delicious cheesey mash. Of course, you can use the cheesey mash with so many other things: top your shepherds' pie with it, make a cheesey champ (see p.134), or serve it with sausage and beans.

SERVES 4

1 tablespoon plain flour
Salt and freshly ground white pepper
4 × 175–225 g (6–8 oz) cod fillets, skinned
1 tablespoon cooking oil
100 g (4 oz) unsalted butter

3–4 tablespoons Fish Stock (see p.221) or water
900 g (2 lb) spinach, picked and washed
Juice of ½ lemon
450 g (1 lb) Mashed Potatoes (see p.133)
100–175 g (4–6 oz) Pecorino, grated

Lightly flour and season the cod with salt and pepper. Heat a frying-pan with the oil and 25 g (1 oz) of the butter. When the pan is hot and the butter bubbling, add the cod and cook for about 3–4 minutes on each side, keeping the pan hot, until the fish is golden brown. Always cook the presentation skin-side down first. When the fish colours, it will show every line of the fillet and also hold the fish together a lot better.

While the fish is cooking, bring the stock or water to the boil with 25 g (1 oz) of butter. Add the spinach leaves and stir for 2–3 minutes. The spinach will cook quickly and create a spinach liquor in the pan. Season with salt and pepper, drain off the spinach and re-boil the liquor. Whisk in the remaining butter to make a spinach butter sauce. Taste and adjust the seasoning if necessary and add the lemon juice to lift the flavour.

Warm the mashed potatoes with 100 g (4 oz) of cheese. Taste and add the remaining cheese, or more if you wish.

Spoon the potatoes on to plates and sit some spinach on top. Arrange the fish on top. You now have a tower of flavours. Pour the spinach butter sauce around and serve.

Fillet of Skate with Red Peppers, Potatoes, Capers and Bayonne Ham

Filleting skate is quite unusual – skate wings are normally cooked on the bone – but it really suits this dish. It's a simple recipe with not too many flavours, just enough to help each other. Bayonne is a cured ham usually made in Orthez near Béarn in south-west France. It has a similar texture to Parma ham but the flavours are different. Bayonne is usually lightly smoked to lift the taste. If you can't find any, substitute Parma ham. Cut the thin slices into 1 cm (½ in) strips ready to fry until crisp.

SERVES 4

2 red peppers
Juice of 1 lemon
6 tablespoons olive oil
Salt and freshly ground white pepper
225–350 g (8–12 oz) new potatoes, peeled, cooked and sliced
2 teaspoons fine capers

4 × 175 g (6 oz) skate fillets
1 tablespoon plain flour
25 g (1 oz) unsalted butter
4–6 slices Bayonne ham, cut into pieces
Mixed salad leaves
2 tablespoons Basic Vinaigrette (see p.241)

Core and halve the peppers lengthways, remove the seeds and cut into 1 cm (½ in) slices lengthways. Mix the lemon juice with 4 tablespoons of olive oil, season with salt and pepper, and pour over the potatoes. Fry the peppers in a little olive oil, colouring and softening slightly, then mix with the potatoes and capers.

Dust the skate with flour, brush with butter and season with salt and pepper. Pre-heat a frying-pan and brush with olive oil. Sit the fillets in the pan, presentation side down, and fry quickly for 2 minutes, then turn and cook for a further minute.

Meanwhile, heat another pan and fry the ham in virtually no fat, cooking and tossing until crisp.

Divide the potatoes and peppers between the plates. Toss the salad leaves in a little dressing and arrange on top. Sit the skate on the leaves and spoon the crisp ham over the top.

Note

Salad leaves are not essential for any of the fish dishes, but they always help the texture.

Fillet of Skate with Red Peppers, Potatoes,
Capers and Bayonne Ham.

Pan-fried Skate with Ratatouille Salad

The skate in this dish is also filleted and shallow-fried.

SERVES 4

2 red peppers
1 green pepper
2 small courgettes
1 large onion, thickly sliced
2 tablespoons olive oil
50 g (2 oz) unsalted butter
2 large, flat mushrooms, sliced
Salt and freshly ground white pepper
1 tablespoon plain flour

4 × 175 g (6 oz) skate fillets
250 ml (8 fl oz) Basic Vinaigrette (see p.241)
6 fresh basil leaves (optional)
1–2 teaspoons Pesto Sauce (see p.235) (optional)
Green salad leaves
1 aubergine, sliced and fried (see p.42)

Core and halve the peppers lengthways, remove the seeds and cut into 1 cm (½ in) slices lengthways. Slice the courgettes at an angle to give oval slices. Fry the onion and peppers in a heavy-based pan in a little olive oil and butter until softened. Add the courgettes and cook for 1 minute then remove from the heat. Cook the mushrooms separately in a very hot pan in a little olive oil, then add to the other vegetables. Season with salt and pepper.

Lightly flour the skate fillets and brush with butter. Heat a frying-pan and brush with oil. Sit the fillets buttered-side down into the pan and fry quickly for 2 minutes on one side, then 1 minute on the other until golden brown.

Mix the vinaigrette with the basil leaves or pesto, if using, and use a little to dress the salad leaves. Add the ratatouille to the dressing and spoon on to plates. Sit the leaves on top and finish with the fish and aubergines.

Variations

Another skate dish that I enjoy is one that is cooked on the bone. The skate is shallow-fried in olive oil and butter for 3–4 minutes on each side until the flesh is crisp and golden brown. Arrange the skate on a plate and surround with some Lemon Butter Sauce (see p.228), finishing with some crunchy brown shrimps and parsley in nut brown butter.

The best shrimps to use are the small, brown variety. To pick them, simply pull off the heads and small tails and leave the rest of the shell on the tail itself. The shell is crispy without being too hard. To make the butter nut brown, heat a frying-pan and add some butter. It should be bubbling and beginning to colour almost immediately. When it's just turning brown but not burnt, add the shrimp tails, a squeeze of lemon juice and season with salt and pepper. Finish with chopped fresh parsley and spoon over the skate.

Sea Bass on Minestrone

This sauce is almost like a minestrone soup, with the flavour of all the vegetables cooked in a tomato liquor. The dish eats well with noodles or with the fish on mashed potatoes. Sea bass is not the only fish that can be used. Red mullet or most white fish will also eat well. A seafood minestrone of scallops, prawns, mussels and cockles is a real winner.

SERVES 4

50 g (2 oz) unsalted butter
1 tablespoon olive oil
2 carrots, diced
1 large onion, diced
2 celery sticks, diced
1 garlic clove, crushed
1 medium courgette, diced
½ leek, diced
2 glasses white wine
150 ml (5 fl oz) Fish Stock (see p.221)

150 ml (5 fl oz) Tomato Coulis (see p.232)
4 × 175–225 g (6–8 oz) sea bass fillets
2 tomatoes, skinned and diced
8–10 fresh basil leaves, cut into squares
12–15 fresh tarragon leaves, cut into squares
1–2 teaspoons Pesto Sauce (see p.235) (optional)

Melt half the butter with the olive oil, then add the carrots, onion, celery and garlic. Cook without colouring for a few minutes. Cook the courgette and leek separately in a knob of butter so that they retain their green colour. Once cooked, allow them to cool, then add them towards the end of cooking. Once the vegetables have softened, add the white wine and boil to reduce until almost dry. Add the stock and boil to reduce by half. Add the tomato coulis and simmer for 10–12 minutes until the sauce has a broth consistency.

Arrange the fish on a buttered and seasoned tray and cook under a hot grill for 5–10 minutes, leaving the skin golden and crispy.

While the fish is cooking, add the tomatoes, herbs, courgettes and leeks to the minestrone, bring to the simmer and add the remaining butter. Finish with the pesto sauce, if liked. Spoon the minestrone sauce into some bowls and sit the fish on top.

Variations

To make this into a more complete meal, cook some noodles and toss in butter. Sit the noodles in the centre of the bowls and spoon the sauce around. Arrange the fish on top.

Try serving the dish with mashed potatoes, leaving out the pesto sauce, and spooning some of the sauce on to the mash before sitting the fish on top and spooning the remaining sauce around.

Stuffed Herrings

This dish eats well on its own simply with a squeeze of lemon or served with a mustard cream sauce (see p.79).

SERVES 4

4 herrings, filleted   Pig's caul (optional)

For the Stuffing

4 medium slices white bread   ¼ teaspoon chopped fresh thyme
1 tablespoon melted butter   ½ teaspoon chopped fresh parsley
1 large onion, finely chopped   25 g (1 oz) bone marrow, finely diced
2 rashers smoked streaky bacon,   (optional)
   finely diced   2 tablespoons shredded suet
½ teaspoon chopped fresh sage   Salt and freshly ground black pepper

Pre-heat the oven to 200–220°C/400–425°F/gas 6–7.

To make the stuffing, remove the crusts from the sliced bread and crumb the slices. Melt the butter, add the chopped onion and cook without colouring for 2–3 minutes. Add the bacon and herbs and continue to cook for 2 minutes. Allow to cool. Mix with the breadcrumbs, diced bone marrow, if using, and suet. Season with salt and pepper. The texture of this stuffing should just hold and bind together if squeezed in your hand.

The herrings should be filleted and as many fine bones removed as possible. Lay out four fillets and divide and spread the stuffing over them. Cover with the other fillets. Before cooking, the fish can be wrapped in pig's caul or in a layer of buttered foil, then pan-fried in a little olive oil and butter until golden brown on both sides. Finish them in the pre-heated oven for a few minutes. Alternatively, if you have used foil, simply bake them in the oven for 12–15 minutes. Once cooked, the caul will be almost invisible. It is used only to hold the fillets together.

Herrings with Spring Onion and Bacon Potato Cakes

These herring fillets are grilled and arranged on top of potato cakes. They can then be served with a wedge of lemon or with a mustard cream sauce.

SERVES 4

8 herring fillets	4 Spring Onion Potato Cakes with bacon
Olive oil or unsalted butter	(see p.133)

For the Mustard Cream Sauce

50 g (2 oz) unsalted butter	A few tarragon leaves
1 shallot, chopped	2 glasses white wine
1 carrot, chopped	300 ml (10 fl oz) Fish Stock (see p.221)
1 celery stick, chopped	50–85 ml (2–3 fl oz) double cream
1 rasher of bacon, chopped	1–3 teaspoons grain mustard

Melt 15 g (½ oz) of butter and cook the vegetables, bacon and tarragon without colouring until they soften. Add the white wine and boil to reduce until almost dry. Add the stock and boil to reduce by half. Add the cream and cook for 8–10 minutes. Strain the sauce and whisk in the remaining butter. Add the mustard a little at a time until you have the right strength.

Meanwhile, brush the herrings with a little oil or butter and cook under a hot grill for 5–6 minutes.

Sit the potato cakes in the centre of the plates, spoon the sauce around and lay the herring fillets on top.

Variations

The potato cake works well using spinach instead of bacon and spring onions (see p.133). Cook 450 g (1 lb) of picked and washed spinach in 25 g (1 oz) of butter for a few minutes until tender, then drain, cool and chop. Add the spinach to the potato mix and proceed as for that recipe. They eat particularly well with fish dishes.

Cooked mushrooms, bacon, onion and many other ingredients can also be added to the potato cakes.

Fish on Spinach with a Cider and Mussel Sauce

I've just called this 'fish' because so many fish work well with this recipe: cod, halibut, sea bass, red mullet, turbot, brill – the list could go on. Make sure whichever fish you choose, it is well filleted with all bones removed. White fish should be skinned as well.

SERVES 4

4 × 175–225 g (6–8 oz) fish fillets
2 tablespoon plain flour
75 g (3 oz) unsalted butter

900 g (2 lb) fresh spinach, picked and washed

For the Mussel Cooking Liquor

15 g (½ oz) unsalted butter
1 onion, roughly chopped
1 carrot, roughly chopped
2 celery sticks, roughly chopped
½ leek, roughly chopped
1 bay leaf (optional)
1 sprig of fresh thyme

1 star anise (optional)
2 glasses dry white wine
600 ml (1 pint) Fish Stock (see p.221) or water
900 g (2 lb) fresh mussels, scrubbed and bearded

For the Cider Sauce

350 g (12 oz) shallots or onions, sliced into rings
25 g (1 oz) unsalted butter
A pinch of saffron (optional)

1–2 bottles dry cider
85–120 ml (3–4 fl oz) double cream
Salt and freshly ground white pepper

To cook the mussels, melt the butter and fry the vegetables, bay leaf, thyme and star anise, if using, for 8–10 minutes without colouring. Add the wine and boil to reduce until almost dry. Add the stock or water, bring to the boil and cook for a few minutes. Add the mussels and bring to the boil, stirring. Once the stock is boiling, the mussels will be opening and cooking. Drain and reserve the cooking liquor. Discard any mussels that have not opened and pick the rest from their shells. Keep them in a few spoonfuls of cooking liquor to keep them moist.

To make the cider sauce, soften the shallots in a knob of butter with the saffron, if using. Add the cider and boil to reduce by three-quarters. Add the mussel stock and continue to reduce by half. Add half the cream, bring to a simmer and simmer for a few minutes. Check for taste and consistency and season with salt and pepper. If the sauce is too thin, reduce a little more. Add a knob or two of butter to enrich the flavour.

The fish should be seasoned and lightly dusted in flour before being pan-fried, or just seasoned if being grilled. Cod will take 3–4 minutes on each side.

While the fish is cooking, melt the butter in a large pan and add the spinach. Cook and stir for 2–3 minutes until tender. Add the mussels to the fish sauce and warm through. Spoon the spinach on to plates and sit the fish on top. Spoon the sauce over the fish, forming a small pile of shallots on top of each fillet.

Poultry and Meat

In this section, I've tried to choose cuts of meat that I feel aren't used often enough, in restaurants or at home. These cuts have a lot more flavour and texture than many of the fine cuts such as fillet of beef. Given a slow cooking process, the wonderful textures are developed to the full. Braised ox cheeks are sensational, so is breast of lamb and haunch of venison. Pork belly is another winner. Left in a spicy marinade for 24 hours, then roasted and glazed with honey, it is transformed into something quite magical. I've also included roasted knuckles and explain how to make good pork scratchings. These again are cuts that we don't seem to use. How often do you make your own pork scratchings? Perhaps it's time you had a go.

Another dish I have included is Home-made Corned Beef. I always used to wonder how corned beef was made and how it got its texture (I'm still not quite sure how they manage to keep that deep red colour!). Well, after reading through several cookery books and plenty of trials I eventually finished with the recipe in this chapter. It is so simple and easy to make. Pork Pie is another homely favourite that we all buy in various sizes from supermarkets, and there are some pretty good ones on offer. But like anything else you can't beat home-made.

You'll also find a few duck dishes and, of course, chicken dishes, one of them with a Scottish theme served sitting on braised pearl barley, which normally features in Scotch broth.

So if you're 'scratching' for an idea to fill your 'belly' just 'knuckle' down and read this chapter!

TOP *Grilled Chicken Breast with Braised Pearl Barley,*
Lemon and Thyme (see p.84).
BOTTOM *Grilled Chicken on Red Wine*
Onions and Mushrooms (see p.85).

Grilled Chicken Breast with Braised Pearl Barley, Lemon and Thyme

This really is a simple dish, not too many ingredients but packed with textures and tastes (see preceding page). Instead of simmering the barley on the stove, it cooks evenly if you put in a pre-heated oven at 180°C/350°F/gas 4.

SERVES 4

1 large onion, finely chopped
175–225 g (6–8 oz) unsalted butter, softened but not melted
900 ml (1½ pints) Chicken Stock (see p.222)
1 leek, sliced or diced

100 g (4 oz) pearl barley
1 teaspoon chopped fresh thyme
Juice of 1–2 lemons
4 chicken breasts
Salt and freshly ground black pepper

To braise the barley, cook the chopped onion in 50 g (2 oz) of the butter, without colouring, until softened. Bring 600 ml (1 pint) of the chicken stock to the boil, add the leeks and cook for 30 seconds. Strain, reserving both stock and leeks. Add the pearl barley to the onions and cook for another 1–2 minutes. Add the stock and bring to the simmer. Cover with a lid and cook over a low heat, stirring continuously, until the barley becomes tender; this will take 30–40 minutes. Add more stock if the barley becomes dry. The remaining 300 ml (10 fl oz) of chicken stock can be boiled until reduced by half to leave you with a good, strong stock.

Mix 100–150 g (4–5 oz) of the butter with the thyme and lemon juice. (This can be made at any time and will keep in the fridge for as long as the butter will last.)

The chicken breasts eat very well if cooked on a grill pan or open barbecue. They can also be pan-fried or cooked under the grill. They will take about 15 minutes.

To finish the barley, add a knob of butter and the leeks and warm through. If there is still a lot of excess chicken stock, simply pour it off. Re-boil the reduced chicken stock, then gradually add and whisk in enough of the lemon and thyme butter until you have a smooth sauce consistency. Season with salt and pepper. Spoon the barley on to the centre of a warmed serving plate and pour the sauce around. Slice the chicken breast through the middle and place on top of the barley.

Grilled Chicken on Red Wine Onions and Mushrooms

This dish is very rich; the flavour of the red onions cooked in red wine eats beautifully (see p.83). Use flat or open cup mushrooms; both have a good flavour and texture. This mushroom and red wine garnish also works well with lamb and beef.

SERVES 4

50 g (2 oz) unsalted butter
8–10 large red onions, sliced
50 g (2 oz) demerara sugar
300 ml (10 fl oz) red wine vinegar
Salt and freshly ground black pepper
1 bottle red wine

2 tablespoons crème de cassis (optional)
8–12 flat or open cup mushrooms
4 chicken breasts
300 ml (½ pint) Red Wine Sauce (see p.230)

Pre-heat the oven to 200°C/400°F/gas 6.

Melt half the butter in a large pan, add the onions and cook for a few minutes without colouring until they begin to soften. Add the sugar and red wine vinegar and boil to reduce until almost dry. Season with salt and pepper. Add the wine and also reduce until almost dry. Season again with salt and pepper and stir in the crème de cassis, if using.

Remove the stalks from the mushrooms and tear off the outer skin from the mushrooms. This is not essential but makes them even more tender. Lay them upside down on a buttered and seasoned tray, brush with butter and season again. Cook under the grill for 4–6 minutes.

Meanwhile, cook the chicken on an open grill or on a grill plate, or just fry in a little butter until golden, then finish in the pre-heated oven for 8–10 minutes. Warm the red wine sauce.

To serve the dish, divide the onions between four bowls (there may well be enough for more!), then sit the mushrooms on top. Carve the chicken through the centre and arrange on top of the mushrooms. Pour the warm sauce around.

Variations

For a lighter sauce, take any of the red onion trimmings from slicing them and cook in a knob of butter for a few minutes until softened. Add 600 ml (1 pint) of red wine and reduce until almost dry. Add 450 ml (15 fl oz) of chicken stock and reduce by half. Strain through a sieve and whisk in 50–75 g (2–3 oz) of unsalted butter. This will give you a lighter red wine sauce that can be blitzed with a hand blender to make it even lighter!

Crispy Roast Duck Breasts with Parsnip Purée

The duck breasts I use for this recipe are called magrets. *This is a duck breast that has been completely removed from the bone and has no wing attached. This breast can then have the skin removed or left on. I prefer to leave the skin on, as this gives a crispy finish.* Magret *duck breasts usually come vacuum-packed from France and are ready to cook. If you can't get* magrets, *simply roast duck breasts still on the carcass, then remove them from the bone once cooked and rested.*

SERVES 4

4 *magret* duck breasts
1 tablespoon vegetable or olive oil
Salt and freshly ground black pepper
4 teaspoons clear honey

450 g (1 lb) parsnips
50 g (2 oz) unsalted butter
1 quantity Cranberry Gravy (see p.238)

Pre-heat the oven to 200°C/400°F/gas 6.

First score the fat on the duck breasts with a sharp knife all the way across (right to left) about 1–2 mm apart. The fat only needs to be scored and not cut through into the flesh. Pre-heat a roasting pan on top of the stove with the oil. Season the scored duck breasts with salt and pepper. Sit the breasts skin-side down into the pan. This will create some spitting from the pan as all water content from the fat will cook out. Once the breasts are cooking fast, turn the heat down to medium and continue to cook the breasts fat-side down until dark and almost burnt. The layer of skin will have cooked right down almost like a confit. Turn the breasts over and finish in the pre-heated oven for 6–10 minutes until the flesh is cooked to medium, depending on the thickness of the breast; a large, thick breast will take 8–10 minutes. Once cooked, the skin will be dark, rich and crispy, almost like duck crackling!

This can now be made even tastier if honey is spooned on top and glazed under the grill. Before serving the breasts, it's best to leave them to rest for 5–10 minutes as this will allow the meat to become more tender.

To make the parsnip purée, peel and split the parsnips lengthways into quarters, and cut out the woody centres. Boil in salted water for about 15 minutes until tender, drain and shake dry. Add the salt and pepper and butter and mash the parsnips. Push through a sieve to get a smooth-textured purée. Serve with the cranberry gravy.

The *magrets* can be left whole or sliced diagonally and arranged on a plate. Serve the parsnip purée separately or shape it between two large spoons to give an oval shape and serve on the plate with the duck. Pour some of the cranberry gravy on to the dish and serve.

Crispy Roast Duck Breasts with Parsnip Purée.

Confit of Duck

This was featured in Rhodes Around Britain. *It's a classic French dish that can also work with goose or pork. In the last book, the duck legs were steeped in a marinade for a few days. Well, this recipe is without the marinade and these duck legs will just be salted for 24 hours before cooking.*

SERVES 4

4 duck legs
2 teaspoons rock sea salt

900 g (2 lb) lard or goose fat, melted

Trim the legs of any remaining feather stalks and remove the knuckle on the underside of the thigh. The skin can also be scored around the top of the drumstick knuckle so this will shrink while cooking and reveal the bone. Salt the legs on the skin side and chill for 24 hours. This will draw any water from the fat and ensure that the skin is crisp when the legs are cooked.

Pre-heat the oven to 160°C/325°F/gas 3.

Sit the legs in a braising dish and cover with melted lard. Bring just to a light simmer, cover with a lid and cook in the oven for 1½–2 hours. To check the legs, remove one from the fat and push the skin side. When you feel the meat is starting to become tender and give, remove from the heat and leave to cool in the fat.

Transfer the legs to a clean dish and cover completely in fat. They will keep chilled almost indefinitely.

To roast the legs, pre-heat the oven to 200°C/400°F/gas 6. Remove the legs from the fat and cut off the end knuckle. Cook in the pre-heated oven for 15–20 minutes until crispy.

Confit of Duck with Orange Sauce and Buttered Spinach

This is a variation on the original confit (see p.88). When salting the duck legs, add the pared rind of one orange and leave it with the legs during the cooking stage. This will help infuse the orange taste. To add even more orange taste to the duck, finely grate the zest of an orange, add it to some clear honey and use to glaze the roasted duck confit and give a sharp orange flavour.

SERVES 4

4 Confit of Duck legs (see p.88)

For the Orange Sauce

300 ml (½ pint) Red Wine Sauce (see p.230)

Pared rind of 1 orange
Juice of 1 orange

For the Buttered Spinach

900 g (2 lb) spinach, picked and washed
50 g (2 oz) unsalted butter

Salt and freshly ground black pepper

To make an orange sauce, start with a red wine sauce. During the cooking of the vegetables, add the orange rind and follow the recipe until the red wine has reduced in volume. Add the orange juice and boil until reduced by three-quarters. Continue with the recipe, adding the veal *jus* or alternative, and cook for 20–30 minutes, pushing the finished sauce through a sieve. The orange sauce is now ready and has a richness helped by the red wine.

To cook the spinach, make sure all excess water has been shaken off the leaves. Melt the butter in a hot pan. Once the butter begins to bubble, add the spinach and stir with a wooden spoon, keeping the pan at a high temperature. The spinach will cook very quickly. After 2–3 minutes, season the spinach with salt and pepper. Drain off any excess liquor and the spinach is ready.

To serve spinach with the duck it's nice to divide the spinach between individual plates or bowls and sit each glazed duck leg confit on top. Just finish by pouring the orange sauce around.

Peppered Confit of Duck with Peppercorn Sauce

Cook the duck legs as for the basic salted recipe (see p.88). Once cooked and removed from the fat, sprinkle finely crushed black peppercorns on top of each leg. The legs can now be roasted and glazed.

SERVES 4

4 Confit of Duck legs (see p.88)

For the Peppercorn Sauce

2 teaspoons green peppercorns, lightly crushed

2 shallots, finely chopped

25 g (1 oz) unsalted butter

50 ml (2 fl oz) brandy

1 glass dry white wine

300 ml (10 fl oz) Veal *Jus* (see p.224) or alternative (see p.226)

150 ml (5 fl oz) double cream

To make a peppercorn sauce, cook the peppercorns and shallots in the butter until just softened. Add the brandy and boil to reduce until almost dry. Add the white wine and boil to reduce until almost dry. Add the veal *jus* or alternative, bring the sauce to the simmer and cook gently for 20 minutes. Add the double cream (it will not curdle) and continue to cook and simmer for a few minutes. You should now have a good sauce consistency with a *café au lait* (milky coffee) colour.

Boiled Collar of Bacon on Mustard Mashed Potatoes with Chive Liquor

I enjoy boiled bacon dishes. The beauty of boiling meat is that it creates its own stock as it cooks, which then becomes the base for the sauce.

Mashed potatoes go well with this dish. I normally don't even tamper with mash, but mustard and bacon are good friends and using them to flavour the potatoes gives them a real bite. You can choose whatever mustard you prefer, but I recommend grain, Dijon or English. My favourite is Dijon mash; not too hot but packed with flavour.

The combination of mustard mashed potatoes and bacon works so well. The potatoes eat equally well with almost any form of pork – roast leg or loin, sausages, or braised belly are just a few.

SERVES 4–6

900 g–1.5 kg (2–3 lb) smoked bacon
collar, rolled and rind removed
1 onion, roughly chopped
2 carrots, roughly chopped
2 celery sticks, roughly chopped
½ leek, roughly chopped
1 bay leaf
1.2–1.75 litres (2–3 pints) Chicken
Stock (see p.222) or water

100 g (4 oz) unsalted butter
Salt and freshly ground white pepper
675–900 g (1½–2 lb) Mashed Potatoes
(see p.133)
About 1 tablespoon Dijon mustard
1 tablespoon snipped fresh chives

Soak the bacon in water for 24 hours before cooking to reduce the salt content.

Sit the bacon in a pan with the vegetables and bay leaf. Cover with the stock or water. Bring to the simmer and continue to simmer for 1–1½ hours. Leave to rest in the liquor for 20–30 minutes.

Drain off 600 ml (1 pint) of the stock, bring to the boil and boil until reduced by half. Whisk in a spoonful of butter at a time to make a creamy sauce; you may find that 75 g (3 oz) is enough. You can use a hand blender to give a creamier consistency. Season with salt and pepper.

Add some mustard to the mashed potatoes a teaspoon at a time, tasting as you go until you have the mustard flavour you want. Spoon the potatoes on to plates. Add the chives to the liquor and spoon round the mash. Carve the bacon, two slices per portion, and arrange on top of the potatoes.

Home-made Pork Pie

A lot of dishes, like this one and the corned beef, sound hard work and you may think there is no point going to all that trouble when there are so many varieties available to buy. In fact, both recipes are very simple, and there's a great feeling of satisfaction when eating the home-made versions. They will never have the artificial pink colour that most bought varieties have. Your pork pie will have a natural colour with just a tinge of pink when finished (see p.62).

The meat I use for this recipe is belly pork, bought already skinned and boned. If you're buying from a butcher then try and get the pork coarsely minced. The pork pie filling must be made before the pastry as hot water crust must be moulded while still warm. The pork pie can be made as a raised pie or flan-style pie. The mould I am using is 18 cm (7 in) diameter by 7.5 cm (3 in) deep. If you don't have a deep pie mould or dish use a 25 cm (10 in) flan ring or mould and follow the same method, but cook for about 1–1½ hours.

To finish the pie, it's best to fill the mould with a jelly made by using a good Chicken Stock (see p.222) boiled to reduce from 1.5 litres (2½ pints) to 900 ml (1½ pints). Alternatively you can use a pork stock by cooking three or four pig's trotters in water for a few hours. This will create its own jelly that can be helped, if needed, with the addition of 15 g (½ oz) of gelatine per 600 ml (1 pint) of stock.

SERVES 8

25 g (1 oz) unsalted butter
2 onions, finely chopped
1 teaspoon chopped fresh sage
1 teaspoon chopped fresh thyme
1 level teaspoon ground mace
½ teaspoon dried English mustard
½ teaspoon dried mixed spice

900 g (2 lb) pork belly, coarsely minced
     or chopped
Salt and freshly ground white pepper
1 egg, beaten
900 ml–1.2 litres (1½–2 pints) jellied
     stock

For the Pastry

600 ml (1 pint) water
100 g (4 oz) lard

450 g (1 lb) plain flour

Melt the butter in a pan. Once the butter begins to bubble, add the chopped onions and cook for a few minutes, without colouring, until just softened. While the onions are still warm, add the sage, thyme, mace, mustard and mixed spice. Allow to cool. Mix the onions and spices with the minced pork, making sure the meat is not over-beaten as this will break down the fat content and texture. Season generously with salt and pepper. It's important to make sure the mix is highly seasoned at the raw stage, as serving it cold will reduce the strength of the seasoning. Leave the filling in the fridge.

Pre-heat the oven to 220°C/425°F/gas 7. Grease a pie mould and place it on a baking sheet.

Bring the water and lard to the boil. Sift the flour with a generous pinch of salt into a bowl, leaving a well in the centre. Pour in the boiling water and lard and stir in the flour to form a dough. Knead lightly by hand (the pastry will be very warm) to give a smooth dough. Keep a quarter of the pastry warm to one side, then work the rest of the pastry on a lightly floured table by hand or with a rolling pin until just under 5 mm (¼ in) thick. Sit the pastry into the mould and work by hand, starting from the centre and gently pushing out to make the pastry thinner and to fill the mould. The finished pastry should be about 3 mm (⅛ in) thick and 5 mm (¼ in) above the top of the mould.

Fill the mould with the pork filling, packing it in just above the top of the mould. Fold the pastry around the top on to the mix and brush with the beaten egg. Roll out the remaining pastry to the same thickness and sit on top of the pie, pressing the edges together and cutting off any excess. Using a small cylinder pastry cutter or piping nozzle, cut a hole in the centre and leave the cutter or nozzle sitting in the hole. The border of the pie can be pinched or pushed with a fork to give a simple patterned edge. Brush the pie with beaten egg.

Bake the pie immediately in the hot oven for 20 minutes, then reduce the oven temperature to 190°C/375°F/gas 5 and cook for a further 1½–2 hours (30 minutes less if you are using a shallow mould). During the first 20 minutes the pie may colour very quickly. Once it's reached golden stage cover lightly with tin foil, only covering the top and not the sides as this will slow down the cooking time.

Test whether the pie is ready either by feeling the filling through the hole in the centre – the mix should be firm to the touch – or inserting a knife into the filling. It should feel tender and the knife will still be clean. Remove the pie from the oven and leave to cool for 30 minutes.

During cooking, the pork filling will have shrunk a little, leaving a border to be filled with jelly. Using a funnel or jug, pour 300 ml (10 fl oz) of the jelly stock into the pie. It will be absorbed by the meat, giving it a moister finish. Leave the pie to finish cooling, by which time the stock will be almost at jelly stage. Pour in the remaining stock until filled and jellied. It's now best to keep the pie in the fridge. See, it was worth it!

Boiled Collar of Bacon with Home-made Sauerkraut

Sauerkraut is a warm pickled cabbage. I used to eat sauerkraut a lot when I lived in Amsterdam in the late 70s and also when visiting my brother who lived in Germany. We would always have grilled bratwurst sausage with sauerkraut in a roll. I think these were the German answer to hotdogs and ketchup!

Sauerkraut is often cooked with bacon to help the flavour. I decided to keep the sauerkraut 'vegetarian'. Serve it with the boiled bacon and mustard seed sauce.

SERVES 4–6

900–1500 g (2-3 lb) bacon collar - boned, skinned, rolled and tied
1 onion, roughly chopped
2 carrots, roughly chopped
2 celery sticks, roughly chopped
1 bay leaf

Chicken Stock (see p. 222) or water to cover bacon
150 ml (5 fl oz) double cream
25 g (1 oz) unsalted butter
1–2 teaspoons mustard seed
Salt and freshly ground white pepper

For the Sauerkraut

1 medium white cabbage, finely shredded
150 ml (5 fl oz) white wine
150 ml (5 fl oz) white wine vinegar

Bouquet garni (2 teaspoons pickling spice, 2 teaspoons lightly crushed juniper berries, a pinch of thyme)
25 g (1 oz) unsalted butter
3 onions, sliced

To start the sauerkraut, place the shredded cabbage in a bowl with the wine and vinegar. Tie the bouquet garni ingredients in a square of muslin and add to the bowl. Leave to marinate for 48 hours, turning occasionally to make sure all the cabbage is marinated. This will give it a good pickly texture and taste.

Soak the bacon in water for 24 hours before boiling. Soaking the bacon releases excess salt content, leaving a better and less salty taste.

Once soaked, remove and wash the collar, and place in a pan with the vegetables, bay leaf and stock or water. Bring to the simmer and continue to simmer for 1-1½ hours. Once cooked, the bacon should be left to rest in the liquor for 20 minutes to relax the meat and make it more tender.

To make the mustard seed sauce, take 600 ml (1 pint) of the cooking liquor and boil to reduce by half. Add the cream and cook for 10 minutes. Add the butter and mustard seed to taste. Check for seasoning with salt and pepper.

To finish the sauerkraut, drain off the liquor and keep to one side. Melt the butter in a pan and add the sliced onions. Allow to cook on a medium heat with no browning until slightly softened. Add the white cabbage, bouquet garni and 2-3 tablespoons of the liquor and cover with a lid. Cook on a medium heat, stirring from time to time. As the cabbage is cooking the pickling liquor will start to evaporate. Add some more liquor a little at a time until the cabbage becomes tender. This will take about 20 minutes. The cabbage should be tender but still have a slight bite. Season with salt and pepper.

To serve the dish, spoon some sauerkraut on to plates. Remove the bacon from the liquor and carve, allowing either one thick or two thinner slices per person. Sit the bacon on top of the cabbage and spoon some liquor over to add some extra moisture to the meat. The dish can now be finished with either extra liquor or the mustard seed cream sauce.

Boiled Collar of Bacon with Home-made Sauerkraut
and mustard seed sauce.

Roast Leg of Pork

Roasting must be one of Britain's most popular cooking methods, especially on Sundays, and pork is a particular favourite. In fact it was one of the meats served at Christmas before turkeys were introduced from America. Roast pork and apple sauce is delicious if the pork has been cooked so that it stays succulent and the skin turns to crackling. You can also mix apple sauce with cranberry sauce to eat with pork (or as a dip for the crackling). When I'm cooking pork I like to sit the leg on pork bones (if you can get them) to protect the meat, or you can use halved onions. The quantity of pork here serves at least ten people but you can, of course, use a smaller cut to suit your own needs.

SERVES 10 or more

3.5–4.5 kg (8–10 lb) leg of pork	4 onions, halved
Lard or cooking oil	600 ml (1 pint) Veal *Jus* (see p.224) or
Salt	alternative (see p.226)
Pork bones (optional)	Salt and freshly ground black pepper

Pre-heat the oven to 200°C/400°F/gas 6–7.

To achieve a good, crisp crackling, the skin on the leg must be scored just deep enough to break through. Brush with lard or cooking oil and sprinkle fairly liberally with salt.

Sit the leg on a few pork bones in a roasting pan. Alternatively, sit the pork on halved onions with the skin left on, placing them face down. The onions not only protect the meat but also slowly cook, absorbing some of the pork juices. Leaving on the skins holds them together. Roast the pork for about 20–30 minutes by which time the pork will have started colouring and crisping. Once it has reached the golden stage, loosely sit a piece of foil on top to prevent it from becoming too dark; don't overtighten it or the leg will create steam underneath and you won't get a crispy crackling. Roast for a further 3 hours, then remove the foil and finish cooking for about 30 minutes until the meat is tender and the crackling has crisped even more. Allow the meat to rest for 20–30 minutes before removing the crackling and carving the meat. A leg of pork this size will always take at least 4 hours to cook.

Once the pork has cooked, pour off any excess fat and add some gravy to collect all the taste from the cooking juices. The onion flavour comes through to lift the gravy. Spoon the onions out of their skins, season with salt and pepper and serve as a vegetable to go with the pork; they are packed with flavour.

Pork Crackling and Scratchings

Roast pork is so good to eat, but I think the best bit is the crackling – good, crunchy, salted pork flavour.

To get good, crispy crackling, the skin has to be scored with a sharp knife just deep enough to break through. Brush the skin lightly with cooking oil or lard, then sprinkle liberally with salt before roasting. The salt will draw any water from the skin and leave a very crisp finish.

I also like to make crackling or scratchings without any meat attached (see overleaf). Ask the butcher for some pork rind, preferably from the loin, and cut off any excess fat underneath. Score and salt the skin and roast in a pre-heated oven at 200°C/400°F/gas 6. The rind will take 30–40 minutes to become crunchy.

To make scratchings, instead of scoring the rind, remove the fat and cut it into 5 mm (¼ in) strips, then sprinkle with salt. Bake in the pre-heated oven for about 30 minutes. It's nice to offer your own scratchings with pre-dinner drinks or use them in a starter for a meal. I like to make a pork scratching and apple salad. Simply quarter some apples and cut again into eight. Fry and toss them in butter, giving a little colour, for 2–3 minutes. Sit them around the plate with warm pork scratchings and mix some snipped fresh chives with Basic Vinaigrette (see p.241) to spoon over. Dress the centre of the plate with mixed salad leaves tossed in dressing.

At Christmas, if you've got some roast pork and crackling left over, use up the crackling in this salad. You can also spoon some Cranberry Sauce (see p.239) into the centre of the plate, dressing the salad leaves on top.

OPPOSITE *Home-made Pork Scratchings in the foreground, and Crackling (see p.97).*

RIGHT *Seared Spicy Pork Belly (see p.100) served with Fried Spinach, Mushrooms and Beansprouts (see p.144).*

BELOW *Hocks and Hands (see p.101).*

Seared Spicy Pork Belly

Pork belly is quite a cheap cut of meat and, I think, highly underrated. Belly slices are wonderful roasted or barbecued, they have a great balance of meat and pork fat content which helps them 'crisp up' during cooking (see preceding page). Well, for this recipe I'm not using the strips but instead squares of belly that have all bone and skin removed. It should be no problem to ask the butcher to cut some for you, but make sure they do remove all skin and bone. The squares you need should be about 7.5 cm (3 in). Teriyaki marinade is available in most large supermarkets; you'll find it near the soy sauce. The pork almost tastes Chinese; it has a good spicy flavour and eats very well with just buttered noodles or with Fried Spinach, Mushrooms and Beansprouts (see p.144).

SERVES 4

4 pork belly squares, prepared as above	4–5 tablespoons of Basic Vinaigrette (see
1 tablespoon olive oil	p.241)
4 teaspoons clear honey	4–6 spring onions

For the Spicy Marinade

150 ml (5 fl oz) teriyaki marinade	2 garlic cloves, sliced
85 ml (3 fl oz) soy sauce	50 g (2 oz) root ginger, finely diced or
1 teaspoon Tabasco sauce	grated
3 tablespoons Worcestershire sauce	

Score the pork belly squares diagonally on the fat side about 3 mm (⅛ in) deep. They should also be scored very lightly underneath. The pork is now ready for marinating.

To make the marinade, simply mix all the ingredients together. Reserve 3 tablespoons to use in the finished dressing, then pour the rest over the pork, turning from time to time. The pork only needs to marinate for 24 hours before cooking. It can, of course, be left longer but this will increase the taste of the spices which could become too strong.

Pre-heat the oven to 200°C/400°F/gas 6.

To cook the pork, heat the olive oil in a roasting pan and add the pork fat-side down over a medium heat. The fat will start to colour almost immediately, giving a rich roasted/seared colour. Continue to colour until quite dark. Turn the pork and cook in the pre-heated oven for about 15–20 minutes. The cooking time will really depend on the thickness of the belly.

Once cooked, spoon the honey on top and glaze under a hot grill. Remove the pork and leave to rest for a few minutes. Mix any excess honey in the pan with the reserved marinade and the vinaigrette dressing and strain through a sieve. Cut the spring onions into small, thin oval pieces. Slice the pork into thin slices and sit in the bowl. Spoon the marinade dressing over and sprinkle with the spring onions.

Knuckles and Hocks, Hands and Scrag Ends

Knuckle, hocks and hands of pork or lamb scrag ends are all 'rough' cuts of meat. Although cheap, they are are packed with flavour, especially when slow roasted and served with gravy (see p.99).

Any of these cuts can be roasted in a medium oven at about 180°C/350°F/gas 4 for 2–2½ hours.

Hand of pork (from the shoulder with the trotter removed) can be bought on or off the bone. Once scored and tied, it is ready to cook. If it's salted and slowly roasted, you will have some very crispy crackling and moist pork underneath. Sliced and served with mustard or apple sauce, it eats really well. It's a brilliant cut to roast and just sit and pick at, or break off crackling, tear the meat and eat it in a French stick sandwich with the bread soaking up all the juices. The same can be done with the other joints.

Scrag ends of lamb are normally casseroled, but a knuckle is for roasting and eats well if glazed with honey and mint.

These are cuts of meat we should use more often. If you have four knuckles of lamb roasted off for a Sunday lunch and you sit them in a bowl and plonk them on the table, I promise you everyone will be excited and delighted by the messy eating!

Breast of Lamb with a Mustard and Herb Crust

Breast of lamb is a cut of meat taken from the belly. It's quite cheap and is packed with flavour. When buying lamb breasts, make sure the lamb has been skinned, boned and any excess fat has been removed. One breast will give you enough for two portions. Once cut in two, roll the lamb lengthways and tie tightly. Lamb breasts are usually roasted or cut into chunks and braised. This dish holds several cooking methods: frying, braising and grilling. It's braised in a stock and can be cooked a few days in advance and kept in its jellied stock. You can add any lamb bones to the stock during cooking to increase the lamb flavour.

SERVES 4

4 portions of lamb breast, rolled and tied
2 tablespoons lamb fat or cooking oil
50 g (2 oz) unsalted butter
1 garlic clove, crushed
1 sprig of fresh thyme
1 sprig of fresh rosemary
A few fresh sage leaves
1 onion, diced
2 carrots, diced
2 celery sticks, diced

½ leek, diced
1.2–1.75 litres (2–3 pints) Chicken Stock (see p.222)
A few lamb bones (optional)
1 teaspoon chopped mixed thyme, sage and rosemary
1 quantity Basic Crumble Mix (see p.114)
2–4 teaspoons Dijon or grain mustard
150 ml (5 fl oz) double cream

Heat a frying-pan and colour the lamb breasts in the fat or oil. Melt half the butter in a braising pan and fry the garlic, herbs and vegetables slowly for a few minutes. Add the stock and lamb bones, if using. Bring to the simmer. Add the lamb breasts and simmer until tender; this will take about 2 hours.

Once cooked, the lamb can be left in the stock and jellied (to use later) or taken out of the stock and finished with the crust.

Add the chopped mixed herbs to the crumble mix and flavour with 1–2 teaspoons of mustard.

Cut the meat into 1 cm (½ in) slices and separate into portions. Push the slices together, just slightly parted at an angle. Top with the herb crust and crisp under a hot grill until golden brown.

To make the sauce, reduce some of the cooking liquor to about 300 ml (10 fl oz). Thicken with the remaining butter and add the double cream, cooking for 5–10 minutes, then add 1–2 teaspoons of mustard and serve.

Breast of Lamb with a Mustard and Herb Crust.

Roast Best End of Lamb with a Parsnip Crumble

The best end of lamb can be ordered from your butcher. If you ask for a pair of best ends and want them chined (split), this will leave you with two best ends, which are like two fillets of lamb with bones attached. If you cut between the bones, this gives you lamb cutlets, and although you can use cutlets for this recipe, I prefer to leave the meat on the bone or as whole fillets before roasting; this will give a totally different taste and texture to the meat. Ask for the lamb to be French-trimmed to the eye of the meat and all fat removed; this means that the bones are clean. You now have the two meat fillets with individual bones attached. Split both through the middle leaving four roasting joints with about three bones attached on each (any excess bones can be cut off).

SERVES 4

2 best ends of lamb, split, French-trimmed and fat removed
Salt and freshly ground black pepper
1 tablespoon cooking fat

1 quantity Parsnip Crumble (see p.117)
300 ml (10 fl oz) Red Wine Sauce (see p.230)

Pre-heat the oven to 200°C/400°F/gas 6.

Season the meat with salt and pepper, then colour it in the cooking fat in a hot pan on top of the stove. Once coloured, transfer to a roasting tin in the pre-heated oven and roast until medium rare. This will take 8–10 minutes, longer if you prefer the lamb a little more cooked. To test the meat, simply press between thumb and forefinger; the meat should feel tender and just give when pressure is applied. The lamb should now be left to rest for about 10 minutes before carving and serving, as this will give the meat a softer texture.

Meanwhile, shape the crumbles in individual rings. Finish in the hot oven or under the grill until golden and crunchy.

Carve between the bones, giving three roasted cutlets per portion. Sit the lamb on top of the individual parsnip crumbles and pour the red wine sauce around.

Roast Best End of Lamb with a Leek and Mustard Crumble

Here is another way of serving the best end of lamb. It's simple to cook. Just follow the lamb preparation and cooking instructions on p.104.

Best ends of lamb also eat well and cook a little quicker if the meat is off the bone. Providing that the lamb is French-trimmed, you can simply cut the meat away from the bone, leaving lamb fillets. Once cooked, these can be sliced either across or lengthways.

The Leek and Mustard Crumble works very well as part of the main dish or as a separate vegetable accompaniment.

SERVES 4

2 best ends of lamb, split, French-trimmed and fat removed
1 quantity Leek and Mustard Crumble (see p.116)

300 ml (10 fl oz) Red Wine Sauce (see p.230)

Roast the lamb (see p.104) and prepare and cook the crumbles in individual rings (see p.119). Arrange the crumbles on a serving plate and sit the roast lamb on top. Pour the red wine sauce around.

Peppered Lamb Fillet with Mint and Caper Sauce

The pepper flavour works really well with the sweetness of lamb, without being overpowering. This dish is packed with lots of different flavours, all of which you can still identify and taste. I use a standard pepper mill to grind the peppercorns, then shake them through a sieve to keep out any large pieces. The lamb fillet I use is from the best end of lamb, which is the joint lamb cutlets come from. All I've done is take the meat completely off the bone.

You don't have to follow this recipe exactly. The same idea can be used for roasting a leg of lamb. Roll it in the pepper and roast it as normal. When the joint is carved, every slice will have a wonderful pepper taste. You can make the same sauce or just flavour your lamb gravy with mint and capers.

Spinach eats very well with this dish, as do Fondant Potatoes (see p.134), which help to mop up the sauce.

SERVES 4

2 fillets from best end of lamb
Black or white peppercorns, crushed
    and sieved

Salt and freshly ground black pepper
1 tablespoon cooking oil or fat

For the Sauce (serves 8–10)

1 large shallot or ½ onion, roughly
    chopped
1 carrot, roughly chopped
1 celery stick, roughly chopped
1 tablespoon unsalted butter
12 fresh mint leaves

2–3 glasses red wine
600 ml (1 pint) Veal *Jus* (see p.224) or
    alternative (see p.226)
1 bay leaf
2 teaspoons fine capers

Pre-heat the oven to 220°C/425°F/gas 7.

To make the sauce, cook the vegetables and bay leaf in the butter until softened and lightly coloured. Add the mint and wine and boil to reduce by three-quarters. Add the *jus* or gravy, bring to the boil and simmer gently for 20 minutes. Season with salt and pepper and strain. The sauce should have a slight mint flavour. Add the capers just before serving.

Meanwhile, cut the fillets in half, giving you four individual portions. Roll them in the crushed peppercorns, shaking off any excess. Season with salt. Heat a roasting pan with the oil or fat and fry the lamb for 1–2 minutes, sealing and colouring all over. Finish the lamb in the pre-heated oven for about 6–8 minutes to cook the lamb to medium. If you want the meat rarer, cook for 5 minutes, or allow 10–12 minutes if you like it well done.

Always allow meat to rest for 5–10 minutes once it is cooked; this will make it more tender to eat. Carve the meat and serve it with the caper *jus*.

Variations

You can make the sauce without the vegetables, just by reducing the red wine with the mint, then adding the *jus*.

Peppered Lamb Fillet with Mint and Caper Sauce served with Fondant Potatoes (see p.134).

Stewed Venison with Vegetables in Red Wine

Venison for stewing should come from the haunch, or you can use neck. I like to cut the meat into large pieces rather than dice. It takes a little longer to cook but the texture and taste are better.

SERVES 4

900 g (2 lb) haunch of venison	A few black peppercorns, lightly
1 tablespoon cooking fat or oil	crushed
450 g (1 lb) onions, sliced	1 bottle red wine
1 sprig of fresh thyme	900 ml–1.2 litres (1½–2 pints) Veal *Jus*
1 bay leaf	(p.224) or alternative (see p.226)
A few juniper berries, lightly crushed	Salt and freshly ground black pepper

For the Garnish

225–275 g (8–10 oz) button onions	4 celery sticks
1 tablespoon cooking fat	6 flat or open cup mushrooms
3 carrots	

Cut the venison into chunks and colour in the fat in a hot frying-pan until completely sealed; remove from the pan. Cook the onions with the thyme, bay leaf, juniper berries and peppercorns for a few minutes. Add half the red wine and boil to reduce until almost dry. Add the *jus* and venison, bring to the simmer, then cook gently for 1½–2 hours, skimming occasionally. Add a tablespoon or two of water if the sauce becomes too thick.

When the stew is almost ready, fry the onions until well coloured. While they are colouring, quarter the carrots lengthways, then cut at an angle into 2 cm (¾ in) pieces. Slice the celery and quarter the mushrooms. Remove the onions from the pan. Add the carrots and celery and colour lightly. Add them to the onions. Add the mushrooms to the pan and fry for a few minutes, then return all the vegetables to the pan and cover with the remaining wine. Boil to reduce until almost dry. The vegetables should now be cooked.

Remove the meat from the sauce and strain the sauce through a sieve. Return the meat to the sauce and check for seasoning with salt and pepper. Add the vegetables to the meat and serve the dish as a stew, or sit the meat in bowls and top with the braised vegetables with the sauce spooned over.

Variations

To enrich the stew, redcurrant jelly can be added to sweeten the sauce; or a spoonful of Dijon or English mustard or a dash of Worcestershire sauce or mushroom ketchup.

The dish can also be turned into a pie by spooning the stew into a pie dish and topping with Shortcrust Pastry (see p.211) or Puff Pastry (see p.212).

You can adapt the recipe to use pheasant, grouse or other game birds.

Another venison dish I enjoy is roasted loin cooked pink, then carved and set on top of a basic Bubble and Squeak (see p.118) or Beetroot Bubble and Squeak (see p.140). Pour some Red Wine Sauce (see p.230) around and the dish is ready.

Venison also eats well with Celeriac and Potato Dauphinoise (see p.136).

Venison Dumplings

You can make these dumplings to serve with the Stewed Venison (see p.108). The offal will give a good, strong, gamey flavour, but if you're not too keen on offal, replace it with 175 g (6 oz) finely chopped or minced black pudding. This will give a strong flavour and can be used in so many other stews or braised dishes, with pork, chicken, duck or lamb.

Serves 4

50 g (2 oz) venison heart, coarsely
    minced
50 g (2 oz) venison liver, coarsely
    minced
50 g (2 oz) venison kidney, coarsely
    minced
2 tablespoons finely chopped onion
    cooked in butter
½ teaspoon chopped fresh sage and
    thyme

100 g (4 oz) shredded suet
225 g (8 oz) self-raising flour
4–5 juniper berries, crushed
A pinch of salt
50–85 ml (2–3 fl oz) water
1 egg
300 ml (10 fl oz) Chicken Stock (see
    p.222) or water

Mix the offal with the chopped onions, herbs, suet, flour, juniper berries and salt. Mix with the water and egg to a reasonably firm dough. Roll into balls and poach in stock or water for 20 minutes. The dumplings can then be added to a stew.

Home-made Corned Beef

You may be surprised to find that this really is a simple recipe. It just needs a little advanced planning as the beef must be soaked for three days before cooking. Corned beef is readily available for everyone, but it's so good to eat it home-made. The texture is similar to a standard corned beef, but this recipe isn't quite as pink in colour. The pig's trotters are optional but will help to create a jelly in the cooking liquor.

Corned beef is lovely to eat with chutney for tea or supper, or to break into pieces to make corned beef hash, fried with onions and potatoes. Hash is good for a cooked breakfast or lunch / supper dish.

The recipe I'm giving is using 2.25 kg (5 lb) of beef. This can be cut down in half but any smaller quantities won't really give you the right balance of beef meat and fat.

SERVES 8

2.25 kg (5 lb) beef flank	2 pig's trotters (optional)
1.75 litres (3 pints) cold water	25 g (1 oz) gelatine leaves or powder
75–100 g (3–4 oz) salt	(optional)

Trim the beef flank of all visible sinews but leave it as a whole piece. Mix the water and 75 g (3 oz) of salt to create brine. To test the strength of the brine, sit a raw new potato in the water; the potato should float. If it won't float, simply add the remaining salt, or more if needed. Sit the beef in the brine and chill for 3 days.

Remove the meat from the brine and wash it, discarding the salt water. Sit the meat in a clean pan with the pig's trotters, if using. Top up with fresh water. Bring to the boil, then simmer for 2½–3 hours, skimming any impurities from the liquor.

Once cooked, remove the meat from the liquor. Drain the cooking liquor through a fine sieve and taste; it should have a good beef flavour. Discard the trotters. Bring the stock to the boil and boil to reduce in volume, and increase its flavour and jelly content. Test the stock/jelly by spooning on to a small plate and placing in the fridge. The jelly must set very firm to enable it to hold the beef together. If it doesn't set firm enough, then add some or all of the gelatine to the mix. Only about 600–900 ml (1–1½ pints) of finished jelly stock will be needed. Make sure you do test the stock/jelly first as the dish is better if only set using natural jellies.

While the beef is still warm, break it down into pieces. The meat will almost separate itself between sinew strips. Any excess sinew can be removed, but make sure that all fat content is kept. The meat can now be pushed through a large mincer plate (5–10 mm/ ¼–½ in) or chopped by hand with the fat. Mix the meat with 600 ml (1 pint) of reduced liquor and check the consistency. The meat should absorb the liquor and be left reasonably loose. If the mix is too firm, add another 300 ml (10 fl oz) of stock. Taste the corned beef before setting in a mould and correct the seasoning with salt and pepper. The mix can now be pressed firmly into a terrine mould or bowl and set in the fridge overnight.

Once set, turn out the corned beef and serve with a salad and pickle, fried for breakfast or turn it into a corned beef hash.

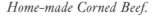

Home-made Corned Beef.

Ox Cheek Stew with Neeps and Tatties

Ox cheeks are an unusual cut of beef with a good, open texture which is ideal for braising or stewing as it enables the beef to absorb all the sauce and liquor. If you can't find a butcher to offer you the cheeks, then just use large pieces of chuck steak. This is similar in texture and will work well in this recipe.

SERVES 4–6

1.1–1.5 kg (2½–3 lb) ox cheeks, trimmed
    of all fat and sinew
Salt and freshly ground black pepper
2 tablespoons cooking fat
2 large onions, sliced
1 small garlic clove, crushed
1 sprig of fresh thyme

1 bay leaf
1 bottle red wine
900 ml–1.2 litres (1½–2 pints) Veal *Jus*
    (see p.224) or alternative (see p.226)
450 g (1 lb) shallots
2 tablespoons unsalted butter

For the Neeps and Tatties

450 g (1 lb) swedes
450 g (1 lb) potatoes

100 g (4 oz) unsalted butter

Season the ox cheeks with salt and pepper. Pre-heat a frying-pan and add a little cooking fat. Fry the cheeks until well coloured on all sides. Remove from the pan and drain off excess fat or liquor. Colour the sliced onions in a braising pan until well coloured. Add the garlic, thyme, bay leaf and half the red wine. Bring to the boil and boil to reduce until almost dry. Add the veal *jus* and ox cheeks and bring to the simmer. Braise the cheeks slowly for 1½–2 hours until tender.

While the cheeks are cooking, split the peeled shallots in half lengthways and cook in a very little butter until well coloured (almost burnt). Add the remaining red wine and reduce until almost dry.

Meanwhile, cook the swedes and potatoes separately in boiling salted water until tender. (I also like to add carrots to this recipe which gives a slightly sweeter flavour.) Drain and leave to dry for a few minutes. Lightly mash the vegetables or stir with a wooden spoon to give a coarse purée. If you prefer a smoother finish push the vegetables through a sieve. Add the butter and season with salt and pepper.

Once the cheeks are cooked, remove them from the sauce and drain the sauce through a sieve. Re-heat the cheeks in the finished sauce and spoon into serving bowls. The shallots can be mixed with the stew or sat on top to finish. Serve with the neeps and tatties.

Vegetarian Dishes

I often find that vegetarian dishes are either not given enough thought or far too much, and are totally overdone with too many garnishes. My feelings about all dishes are that nothing should be added unless it's going to enhance the flavours.

All our eating habits and moods change. Whenever I have a 'pub lunch' (and it's not often enough!) I always go for the vegetarian dish of the day. It's usually a vegetable cottage pie, pasta dish or quiche and I always enjoy it.

A quiche is easy and simple to make, so I decided to make a feature with vegetarian tarts all using the same base mixture. The scope is endless; so many different flavours can be added to give totally different results. Another dish that also has a lot of variety is a vegetarian crumble, these can be complete meals on their own or accompaniments to a main course dish.

Basic Crumble Mix

This recipe really couldn't be simpler. It's just two ingredients held together with butter and, of course, seasoned with salt and pepper. The nicest thing about it is that it lends itself to so many flavour combinations: from parsley and lemon to horseradish or mustard and herbs. If you are using additional flavours, add them before stirring in the shallot butter. All these flavours work well with fish, meat or vegetarian dishes.

It's best to use sliced bread that is 24 hours old, as this will firm the bread slightly and prevent the crumbs from becoming doughy.

SERVES 4

6–8 slices white bread
25–50 g (1–2 oz) unsalted butter, melted
2 large shallots or ½ onion, finely
    chopped

Salt and freshly ground black pepper

Remove and discard the crusts from the bread and cut into quarters. The quickest way to turn these slices into crumbs is to blitz in a food processor. If you don't have a food processor, simply push the slices through a metal sieve.

Melt the butter with the chopped shallots and bring to the simmer, remove from the heat and leave to cool.

Gradually spoon some of the shallot butter into the crumbs, mixing all the time. The mix will be ready when it holds once pressed together, but it should still stay free-flowing.

Use the crumble as directed in the following recipes.

Spinach and Horseradish Crumble

This crumble recipe has the sharp tang of horseradish which goes so well with the buttered spinach. I've used this with lots of dishes, especially roast meats, grilled herrings or salmon.

SERVES 4

1 quantity Basic Crumble Mix (see p.114)

2 tablespoons horseradish sauce

25–50 g (1–2 oz) unsalted butter

900 g (2 lb) fresh spinach, washed and picked

Salt and freshly ground white pepper

Freshly grated nutmeg (optional)

Follow the recipe for the basic crumble, only using a maximum of 25 g (1 oz) of butter. Mix the horseradish sauce with the crust mix and taste, adding a little more if you like a stronger taste.

Cook the spinach at the last moment for the maximum taste, and cook it quickly. Heat a large, shallow pan and add the butter. As soon as the butter is bubbling, add the spinach, increasing the heat. Stir lightly with a wooden spoon to ensure even cooking. The leaves will immediately start to break down and will be cooked within 1–2 minutes. Season with salt, pepper and nutmeg, if using. If the spinach has produced a lot of liquor, drain it into a small pan and boil to reduce, then return it to the spinach. Spoon the spinach into a buttered flameproof vegetable dish and cover with the horseradish crumble mix. Finish under the grill until golden brown.

Variations

Herbs can be added to the crumbs: parsley, tarragon, thyme or sage will all work well.

You can reserve the spinach liquor and blitz in a little butter with a hand blender to create a spinach butter sauce. This works well with grilled herrings.

It is best to make this dish at the last minute, but there is an alternative. Plunge the spinach into boiling salted water for about 1–2 minutes until just tender, then drain and refresh in ice-cold water. Squeeze any excess water from the spinach, add a knob of softened butter and season with salt, pepper and nutmeg. Spoon into a flameproof, microwave vegetable dish and cover with the crust mix. Before serving, re-heat the whole dish in the microwave, then colour and crisp under the grill.

Leek and Mustard Crumble on Cheesey Mashed Potatoes

This recipe can be adapted to so many dishes, plus it's a complete vegetarian meal on its own. You can even make it without the cheesey mashed potatoes and still have a great accompaniment to many simple meat or fish dishes.

SERVES 4–6

100 g (4 oz) unsalted butter
2 onions, sliced
150 ml (5 fl oz) Vegetable Stock (see p.223)
450–675 g (1–1½ lb) leeks, split and sliced
2 teaspoons chopped fresh parsley
2 teaspoons chopped fresh tarragon

1 quantity Basic Crumble Mix (see p.114)
2 teaspoons grain mustard
450–675 g (1–1½ lb) Mashed Potatoes (see p.133)
100–225 g (4–8 oz) Cheddar, grated
Salt and freshly ground white pepper

Pre-heat the oven to 200°C/400°F/gas 6.

Melt 25 g (1 oz) of butter in a pan. When the butter begins to bubble, add the sliced onions and cook for a few minutes over a medium heat until slightly softened. Add the stock and bring to the boil. Add the leeks, return to the boil and cook for 30 seconds. Strain off the leeks and onions, keeping the stock. Boil the stock until reduced by half to increase its flavour.

To finish the crust mix, add the chopped parsley and tarragon to the mix, then add the grain mustard to taste.

Warm the mashed potatoes with 100 g (4 oz) of the grated Cheddar until melted. I prefer the cheese flavour to be stronger, so continue to stir in the cheese until you have the flavour you want. Check for seasoning with salt and pepper.

Spoon the mashed potatoes into a large vegetable dish. Warm the onions and leeks in a teaspoon of the vegetable liquor, then spoon over the potatoes, and finish with the mustard seed crumble mix. Finish in the pre-heated oven or under a hot grill for about 10 minutes until the crumble is golden and crunchy.

To make the sauce, re-heat the reduced vegetable liquor and vigorously whisk in the remaining butter to give an almost creamy consistency. If you have an electric hand blender, just blitz the liquor and butter together; this will really bind the sauce. Season with salt and pepper and serve with the crumble.

Variations

Try different cheeses instead of the Cheddar; a smoked cheese tastes good.

The filling can also be left to cool and chilled and either re-heated through in the oven or microwaved.

Parsnip Crumble

If you want to make this in individual portions, divide the parsnips between four or six 10 cm (4 in) buttered flan rings, pushing the parsnips in so they almost mould together.

Serves 4–6

900 g (2 lb) parsnips	1 quantity Basic Crumble Mix (see
2 tablespoons unsalted butter or cooking	p.114)
fat	1 teaspoon chopped fresh thyme
Salt and freshly ground black pepper	1 teaspoon chopped fresh rosemary

Pre-heat the oven to 220°C/425°F/gas 7.

Peel and split the parsnips lengthways into quarters, and cut out the woody centres. To roast the parsnips, pre-heat a roasting tray on top of the stove with a little butter or cooking fat. Add the parsnips and colour until golden brown. Season with salt and pepper. Roast in the pre-heated oven for 15–20 minutes, turning occasionally for even colour and cooking. For this particular dish, the parsnips need to be slightly overcooked to help shape them into the moulds and also give the centre a purée texture while the outside remains crispy.

To make the crumble, add the herbs to the crumbs before moulding with the shallot/onion butter. Spoon the crumble over the top of the parsnips in a vegetable dish or individual rings and finish in the hot oven or under a hot grill until golden and crunchy.

Roast Parsnip and Chestnut Crumble on Bubble and Squeak

This dish makes a great alternative vegetarian Christmas lunch that includes all those familiar traditional flavours (see p.63). It can be eaten on its own, or you can use this recipe as your total accompaniment to roast turkey. It can also be made any time of the year (perhaps leaving out the chestnuts!).

You can buy cooked chestnuts in tins or frozen. If you are using fresh chestnuts in shell, you will need about 225 g (8 oz). Pre-heat the grill. Pierce the chestnuts once with a knife, then grill for about 15 minutes until the skins split. Leave to cool, then peel and chop roughly.

This dish eats very well with cranberry sauce, especially my recipe flavoured with orange and port (see p.239).

I like to make this in individual moulds, but if you don't have them, don't worry. It works just as well and looks really tasty in a large vegetable dish. Just make the bubble and squeak in the traditional way in a large frying-pan, colouring on both sides, and then spooning into the vegetable dish in the same way.

If you have decided to make this in advance and have chilled it before finishing with the crumble, then it's best to re-heat in the oven for 30 minutes before adding the crumble. Return the dish to the oven or grill until it turns golden brown.

SERVES 4

For the Parsnips

15 g (½ oz) unsalted butter
2 tablespoons cooking oil
1.1 kg (2½ lb) peeled parsnips, split into quarters lengthways and cored

Salt and freshly ground black pepper
1 tablespoon clear honey (optional)

For the Bubble and Squeak

675 g (1½ lb) Brussels sprouts
50 g (2 oz) unsalted butter
2 large onions, thinly sliced

675 g (1½ lb) Mashed Potatoes (see p.133), made without milk or cream

For the Crumble

25 g (1 oz) unsalted butter
1 large onion, finely chopped
100–175 g (4–6 oz) cooked chestnuts,
    chopped (optional)
2 tablespoons chopped fresh parsley
2 tablespoons chopped fresh sage

1 tablespoon chopped fresh thyme
175 g (6 oz) fresh white breadcrumbs

Watercress sprigs to garnish
1 quantity Vegetable Butter Sauce (see
    p.228) to serve

Pre-heat the oven to 200°C/400°F/gas 6 and grease a baking sheet.

Heat the butter and oil in a roasting pan on top of the stove, add the parsnips and fry on a medium heat, turning the parsnips until golden. Season with salt and pepper, then transfer to the pre-heated oven and roast for 15–20 minutes. The parsnips will now be deep golden brown and crispy, but almost overcooked and soft inside. While still hot, lightly toss in the honey, if using.

To make the bubble and squeak, cook the sprouts in boiling salted water until tender. Cool and refresh in cold water. Once cold, halve lengthways and slice. In a small pan, melt 25 g (1 oz) of butter and gently cook the onions for 4–5 minutes until softened. Leave to cool. Mix the onions with the sprouts, then add the mashed potatoes a spoonful at a time until a firm texture is achieved. Season with salt and pepper.

If you wish to make these into individual crumbles, grease four to six 10 cm (4 in) pastry cutters and divide the mix between them. Heat the remaining butter in a frying-pan and place the squeaks, still in the cutters, into the pan and fry until golden brown underneath; this will take 4–5 minutes. Once ready, place the moulds on the greased baking sheet, cooked side down. Spoon the cooked parsnips on top of the bubble and squeak, lightly pressing down. You can leave the recipe to cool then chill at this stage and finish before serving.

To make the crumble (almost a Christmas stuffing), heat the butter in a small pan and cook the onion over a medium heat for 2–3 minutes. In a large bowl mix the chestnuts, if using, chopped herbs and crumbs and season with salt and pepper. Add the onion and butter and mix together.

Sprinkle the crumble mix on top of the warm bubble and squeak and parsnips and place in the pre-heated oven for 10–12 minutes (double the time if it has been chilled). The dish should now be hot all the way through and can be finished under a hot grill until golden and crunchy. Remove the rings, arrange the bubble and squeak on plates, garnish with watercress and serve with the vegetable butter sauce.

Savoury Tarts

I could make this almost a separate chapter; the combinations go on and on. These tarts make perfect vegetarian dishes as well as just good starters, main courses or snacks. They have a different texture to traditional quiche lorraine and are very easy to make. You can make this in one large flan ring or as individual tartlets.

The basic tart mix is made up of eggs, cream and cheese. I am using grated, fresh Parmesan to give a good, strong flavour and a smooth consistency. Other cheese can be used, from Cheddar and Gruyère to a smoked cheese – Italian Pecorino works well. When cooking the tart mix, it's important not to let it boil or this will scramble the eggs.

You can use puff or shortcrust pastry for your tarts, both of which are available at most supermarkets. I prefer puff pastry as it gives a lighter, cleaner finish. Turn to p.212 for details on how to make and blind bake puff pastry cases.

Basic Tart Mix

This recipe has almost unlimited combinations. It also has to be one of the quickest and easiest tart mixes to make. The quantity of this basic recipe can easily be adjusted, it really depends on what the filling is going to be. This amount will be enough for six 10 cm (4 in) individual or one 25 cm (10 in) case.

SERVES 6

300 ml (10 fl oz) double cream	2 eggs, beaten
2 heaped tablespoons freshly grated Parmesan	Salt and freshly ground black pepper

Beat the cream, Parmesan and eggs and season with salt and pepper. The mix is now ready to use.

Almost any filling can be bound and finished with this mix, but all the fillings must be previously cooked or blanched before adding to the Parmesan cream. The filling can then be warmed until it thickens, making sure it does not boil as this will scramble the eggs. The mixture can then be spooned into tart cases and cooked in the oven until set, or chilled to be used later.

Onion and Mushroom Tart with a Parsley Garlic Crust

This tart cooks almost like a crumble with the garlic and parsley crust (see overleaf). It eats very well with a tomato salad or Tomato and Mustard Seed Salad (see p.126).

SERVES 6

25 g (1 oz) unsalted butter
1 tablespoon olive oil
4 onions, sliced
225 g (8 oz) button mushrooms, sliced
Salt and freshly ground black pepper
1 quantity Basic Tart Mix (see p.120)

6 × 10 cm (4 in) or 1 × 25 cm (10 in) Puff Pastry cases, blind baked (see p.212)
½ quantity Basic Crumble Mix (see p.114)
2 tablespoons chopped fresh parsley
1 large garlic clove

Pre-heat the oven to 200°C/400°F/gas 6.

Melt the butter with the olive oil, add the sliced onions and cook over a moderate heat for 2–3 minutes. Add the button mushrooms, increasing the heat, and cook for a further 2–3 minutes. Season with salt and pepper. Add the basic tart mix and cook without boiling for 15–20 minutes. The filling is now ready to use, or it can also be cooled and kept chilled for a few days.

Spoon the mix into the cooked pastry cases and finish in the pre-heated oven for 15–20 minutes. One large flan will need 30–35 minutes.

While the tart is cooking, start to make the crumble topping. Add the crushed garlic to the shallots in the original recipe and cook in the butter. Add the chopped parsley to the breadcrumbs and finish as per recipe.

Once the flans are cooked, sprinkle the parsley and garlic crust on top, covering the flan completely. Finish slowly under a grill until golden and crispy.

Clockwise, starting top left: Onion and Mushroom Tart with a Parsley Garlic Crust (see above); Parsley, Shallot and Onion Tart with Tomato and Mustard Seed Salad (see p.126); Ratatouille Tart with Crispy Aubergine and Tomato Dressing (see p.127); Wild Mushroom Tart (see p.125); Provençale Tart (see p.124).

Provençale Tart

This is similar to the Ratatouille Tart (see p.127), using onions, courgettes, red and green peppers, but they both eat very differently with different textures, tastes and sauces. You can make the filling in advance and keep in the fridge for a few days. The tart eats very well with a pesto mayonnaise sauce (see preceding pages).

SERVES 6

25 g (1 oz) unsalted butter
2 onions, sliced
1 large red pepper, sliced
1 large green pepper, sliced
1 garlic clove, crushed
Salt and freshly ground black pepper
1 quantity Basic Tart Mix (see p.120)

2 courgettes, sliced
1–2 tablespoons olive oil
4–5 plum or salad tomatoes, sliced
6 × 10 cm (4 in) or 1 × 25 cm (10 in)
    Puff Pastry cases, baked blind (see
    p.212)

For the Sauce

1 tablespoon Pesto Sauce (see p.235)   150 ml (5 fl oz) Mayonnaise (see p.242)

Pre-heat the oven to 200°C/400°F/gas 6.

Melt the butter in a pan and add the onions, peppers and garlic. Season with salt and pepper and cook for 4–5 minutes over a moderate heat until the vegetables begin to soften. Add the basic tart mix and warm through gently until the mix thickens; this will take 15–20 minutes. Do not allow the mix to boil.

Fry the courgette slices in a hot frying-pan in a little olive oil for 20–30 seconds, giving the courgettes some colour. Spoon the filling into the tartlet case or cases, then decorate the top of the flans with slices of courgettes and tomato, making two alternating lines of each. Cook in the pre-heated oven for 15–20 minutes for individual tarts or 30–35 minutes for one flan until it sets to the touch. If the mix has been kept chilled it will take an extra 8–10 minutes to cook.

Mix the pesto with the mayonnaise and check seasoning with salt and pepper. Spoon the mixture on to the centre of the plates or bowls and sit the tart on top. Finish with a trickle of olive oil.

Note

The quantity of pesto to mayonnaise is only a guideline – more pesto can be added for a stronger taste. Shop-bought pesto and mayonnaise can be used.

Wild Mushroom Tart

Wild mushrooms are becoming increasingly readily available in our grocers and supermarkets. The variety also seems to be growing. Oyster mushrooms, ceps, trompettes de la mort and chanterelles can all be used in this tart, as a mixture or just using one type.*

If you can't find fresh wild mushrooms, you should have no problems locating some dried wild mushrooms. These just have to be soaked in cold water until they soften, then you can use them as the fresh ones. Keep the soaking water, sieve it to remove any impurities, then boil it until reduced. This reduced liquor will increase the wild mushroom flavours.

The tart eats very well with a green salad and a dressing made with olive oil and chopped black olives and chives (see pp.122–23).

SERVES 6

100–150 g (4–6 oz) open cup or flat mushrooms, sliced
175 g (6 oz) fresh wild mushrooms OR 100 g (4 oz) soaked dried wild mushrooms
25 g (1 oz) unsalted butter

2 tablespoons olive oil
2 large onions, sliced
1 small garlic clove
1 quantity Basic Tart Mix (see p.120)
6 × 10 cm (4 in) or 1 × 25 (10 in) Puff Pastry cases, blind baked (see p.212),

Pre-heat the oven to 200°C/400°F/gas 6.

Fresh wild mushrooms must be washed and cleaned. If you are using oyster mushrooms, these can be torn by hand into strips. Any large mushrooms should be trimmed and sliced. If you are using dried mushrooms, soak them in water until soft, then drain.

Melt the butter with 1 tablespoon of olive oil in a large pan. Add the onions and cook for a few minutes without colouring. Add the garlic and mushrooms. Increase the heat and stir for a few minutes. If some liquor has been formed from the mushrooms with the onions, drain off any excess liquid to a separate pan and boil until reduced.

Add the mushroom and onion mix to the basic tart mix with any reduced liquor. Warm and thicken the tart mix for 15–20 minutes over a low heat, without overheating or boiling. Spoon the mix into the pastry rings and finish in the pre-heated oven for 20 minutes for individual tarts or 30–35 minutes for one flan. Once cooked and just set, brush with the remaining olive oil and serve.

Parsley, Shallot and Onion Tart with Tomato and Mustard Seed Salad

Continental flatleaf parsley has more flavour than ordinary parsley. It looks similar to fresh coriander. If you can't find any, just use ordinary parsley. You can make one tart or six individual ones (see pp.122–23).

SERVES 6

6 x 10 cm (4 in) or 1 × 25 cm (10 in) Puff Pastry cases, blind baked (see p.212)
1 large bunch of flatleaf parsley
1 tablespoon olive oil
25 g (1 oz) unsalted butter

3 large onions, sliced
225 g (8 oz) shallots, sliced
1 garlic clove, crushed
1 quantity Basic Tart Mix (see p.120)
Salt and freshly ground white pepper

For the Salad

6 ripe plum or salad tomatoes
1 teaspoon grain mustard or to taste

4 tablespoons Basic Vinaigrette (see p.241)
1 teaspoon snipped fresh chives

Pre-heat the oven to 200°C/400°F/gas 6.

Pick the flatleaf parsley from the stalks and blanch in boiling salted water for 45 seconds. Drain and refresh with cold water. Squeeze out any excess water from the parsley and lightly chop.

To cook the onions and shallots, warm the olive oil and butter until the butter begins to bubble. Add the onions, shallots and garlic and cook over a moderate heat without colouring until softened. Remove from the heat and allow to cool. Once cooled, mix with the chopped parsley and the basic tart mix. Season with salt and pepper. Warm the tart mix through gently until thickened.

Spoon the tart mix into the pastry cases and bake in the pre-heated oven for 30–35 minutes for one flan or 15–20 minutes for individual tarts.

To make the salad, eye the tomatoes and cut into eight pieces. Season with salt and pepper. Add the mustard to the vinaigrette, then add the snipped chives. Mix the dressing with the salad and serve with the warm tart.

Ratatouille Tart with Crispy Aubergine and Tomato Dressing

We all like ratatouille; it has that Italian theme and is packed with different flavours. Well I've taken all these flavours and put them into a tart case bound with my basic tart mix (see pp.122–23). One of the most exciting tastes in this dish is the aubergines. They eat like home-made aubergine crisps!

SERVES 6

3 tablespoons olive oil
25 g (1 oz) unsalted butter
2 onions, sliced
1 garlic clove, crushed
Salt and freshly ground black pepper
1 large red pepper, seeded and thinly sliced
1 large green pepper, seeded and thinly sliced
1 quantity Basic Tart Mix (see p.120)

2 courgettes
6 × 10 cm (4 in) or 1 × 25 cm (10 in) Puff Pastry cases, blind baked (see p.212)
1 large aubergine
100 g (4 oz) plain flour
1 teaspoon cayenne pepper
Oil for deep-frying
1 quantity Tomato Dressing (see p.233)

Pre heat the oven to 200°C/400°F/gas 6.

Heat a large pan and add 1 tablespoon of oil and the butter. When the butter starts to bubble, add the onions and crushed garlic, season with salt and pepper and cook for a few minutes until softened. Remove the onions from the pan and add a dash more olive oil to the pan. Allow the oil to heat, then fry the peppers, seasoned, until lightly coloured. Return the onions to the pan, add the basic tart mix and thicken on the stove for about 15–20 minutes over a low heat. Do not allow to boil.

Split the courgettes lengthways and cut into thin slices. Quickly shallow fry in a little oil in a hot pan until golden; about 1–2 minutes. These can now be added to the mix.

Spoon the mixture into the flan cases and finish in the pre-heated oven for 15–20 minutes for individual tarts or 30–35 minutes for one flan. The tart should only be set to the touch. If the mix has been chilled, it will take a further 8–10 minutes to cook.

Split the aubergine lengthways, then cut across into thin slices. Mix together the flour and cayenne pepper with a pinch of salt. Dust the aubergine, then fry in hot deep oil until golden and crispy.

Place the tart in the centre of a serving plate and spoon some tomato dressing around. Sit the aubergine crisps on top of the tart and serve.

Stuffed Mushrooms

Stuffed mushrooms can be made so many different ways, with a range of fillings, toppings and textures. They work very well as vegetarian starters or main courses, or you can use prawns, mussels, bacon or other fish or meat ingredients. Rather than give you a basic recipe, I thought I would just share a few ideas.

I like to use large, flat mushrooms which have a good meaty texture and taste. It's best to half cook them before adding any filling. They can then be stuffed, topped and baked. I always half-cook the mushrooms on a seasoned and buttered tray under the grill with a trickle of olive oil.

My favourite filling is cooked spinach. You can flavour this with garlic, leeks or even crispy smoked bacon pieces, then top the spinach with either a herb crust (see p.121) or thick slices of grated Cheddar or Gruyère. Bake the mushrooms in a pre-heated oven at 200°C/400°F/gas 6, then finish under the grill. These eat very well as a starter.

Other good fillings are a small, diced ratatouille finished with Parmesan or Stilton and spinach or just Stilton and breadcrumbs, leeks with mustard and Cheddar, or sliced tomatoes topped with Welsh rarebit mix (from Rhodes Around Britain*).*

Turn to p.130 to see how good they look.

Vegetarian Stir-fry

This really is tasty to eat as a starter or main course. It also works well with some other fish or meat dishes.

SERVES 4

2 onions, sliced
2 tablespoons olive oil
50 g (2 oz) unsalted butter
225 g (8 oz) beansprouts, blanched in boiling water
225 g (8 oz) cup mushrooms, sliced
450 g (1 lb) spinach, washed and torn
175 g (6 oz) cooked fine spaghetti/noodles

1 tablespoon clear honey
2 tablespoons Spicy Marinade (see p.100)
Juice of 1 lime
Salt and freshly ground black pepper
6 spring onions, diagonally sliced

The first thing is to start to cook the onions in a wok with the oil and butter for a couple of minutes. Add the blanched beansprouts and sliced mushrooms and continue to cook over a moderate heat for 2 minutes. Add the spinach and cook for a minute until just wilted. Add the cooked spaghetti or noodles and cook for a further 2 minutes. Add the honey, marinade and lime juice. Check for seasoning with salt and pepper, divide between four bowls and spoon over the liquor. Finish with the sliced spring onions.

ABOVE *Making the Vegetarian Stir-fry (see p.129).*

OPPOSITE *In the foreground are mushrooms stuffed with spinach with a herb crust and behind are mushrooms stuffed with ratatouille (see p.128).*

Vegetables

Some of these recipes will tell you how to get the maximum flavour from a bowl of sliced carrots, peas or beans.

There's all sorts of potato dishes, including one of my favourites, Irish Champ – lovely mashed buttery potatoes with spring onions. I've also included a shocking pink recipe, Beetroot Bubble and Squeak. It's not just the colour that shocks, it's the flavour, too. The Beetroot Fritters are crispy and golden, the Spring Onion Potato Cakes are full of textures and as for the stir-fry – you won't believe how quick and easy it is.

Mashed Potatoes

I find Maris Piper are one of the best varieties for making mashed potatoes – then all you need to add is a little care.

SERVES 4–6

900 g (2 lb) potatoes, quartered
Salt and freshly ground white pepper
100 g (4 oz) unsalted butter

120 ml (4 fl oz) double cream or milk
Freshly grated nutmeg

Boil the potatoes in salted water until tender, about 20–25 minutes depending on size. Drain off all the water and replace the lid. Shake the pan vigorously which will start to break the potatoes. Add the butter and cream or milk a little at a time, while mashing the potatoes. Season with salt, pepper and nutmeg. The potatoes will be light, fluffy and creamy.

Spring Onion Potato Cakes

This is a basic recipe which can be developed to suit so many other dishes. I like to add diced, smoked bacon which goes well with the spring onions, and I serve this with a grilled herring dish (see p.79). It's also good to keep this a vegetarian dish so why not just add grated cheese and onion and serve with a good tomato salad.

SERVES 4

25 g (1 oz) unsalted butter
1 large bunch of spring onions, finely
   diced
350 g (12 oz) Mashed Potatoes (see
   p.133), made without cream or milk

2 tablespoons olive oil
2 egg yolks
Salt and freshly ground white pepper
3 tablespoons plain flour

Melt half the butter and fry the spring onions quickly. While the mashed potatoes are still warm, add the olive oil, egg yolks and spring onions and season with salt and pepper. Fold in the flour. The mix can now be divided into four discs about 1–2 cm (½–¾ in) thick and pan-fried in the remaining butter and a little extra olive oil. The cakes will take about 3–4 minutes on either side.

It is always best to pan-fry the cakes as soon as the mix is ready. This will prevent it from becoming soggy. Once cooked, the cakes can be kept and chilled, then baked through in the oven when needed. However, to eat them at their best, eat as soon as cooked.

Fondant Potatoes

These are potatoes that traditionally are shaped into barrels and then braised in chicken stock until all the stock has reduced and been absorbed. The potato is then packed with flavour. Well, I'm not changing this recipe too much, except the potatoes don't need to be shaped, they are just peeled and halved (see p.107).

SERVES 4

2 large baking potatoes, peeled and halved lengthways
600 ml (1 pint) Chicken Stock (see p.222) or Vegetable Stock (see p.223)
Salt
25 g (1 oz) unsalted butter

Pre-heat the oven to 200°C/400°F/gas 6.

Sit the potatoes in a small, buttered baking tray or flameproof dish. Pour in the stock, filling just three-quarters up the sides of the potatoes. Brush the potatoes with butter and lightly season with salt. Bring the stock to the simmer on top of the stove, then transfer to the pre-heated oven for 30–40 minutes. During this time the potatoes will be absorbing the stock. If the stock becomes almost dry, simply check the potatoes with a knife; they may be ready. If not, just add a little more stock, about 5 mm (¼ in) and continue to cook.

For the last 10 minutes of cooking time, brush the potatoes with butter to help give them a nice golden colour. They can also be finished under a hot grill.

Champ

I'm not quite sure if champ comes from Scotland or Ireland. I first experienced it in Northern Ireland, but have read in several books that it was first made in Scotland. It's one of those recipes that everybody believes their way is the only way to make it. Well, I'm not going to say that this is the way; I'll sit on the fence and just give you my version of champ!

The dish can be eaten on its own or just as a potato dish with boiled ham or bacon. I normally serve it with a boiled bacon collar, just spooned over with its cooking liquor and served with English mustard.

SERVES 4

150 ml (5 fl oz) milk
225 g (8 oz) spring onions, sliced
450–675 g (1–1½ lb) Mashed Potatoes
(see p.133), made without cream or
butter

Salt and freshly ground white pepper
A pinch of freshly grated nutmeg
(optional)
100–175 g (4–6 oz) unsalted butter

Bring the milk to the simmer with the spring onions. Add this to the mashed potatoes and season with salt and pepper. I like to add a pinch of nutmeg. Add half the butter to give a creamier texture. Spoon the potatoes into a bowl and make a well in the middle. The remaining butter can now be sat in the centre. The champ is ready.

Variations

You can substitute chives, nettles, onions or even peas for the spring onions. You can also make red champ with pieces of cooked beetroot added to the potatoes.

Champ.

Celeriac and Potato Dauphinoise

This is a French potato dish that has undergone one or two changes. The flavours are lovely and this eats well with most of the main courses.

SERVES 4

2 large onions, sliced
50 g (2 oz) unsalted butter
600 ml (1 pint) double cream
1 garlic clove, crushed

Salt and freshly ground black pepper
450 g (1 lb) potatoes, thinly sliced
1 large celeriac, peeled and thinly sliced

Pre-heat the oven to 180–190°C/350–375°F/gas 4–5.

Cook the onions in half of the butter for 2–3 minutes without colouring, then allow to cool. Bring the cream to the boil with the crushed garlic and remaining butter and season with salt and pepper. Arrange the onions, potatoes and celeriac in layers in a large ovenproof dish, making sure the potatoes are on the top and bottom. Overlap the top layer of potatoes to give a neater finish. Pour over the cream, making sure the potatoes are covered. Bake in the pre-heated oven for 45–60 minutes until the vegetables are tender and have absorbed the cream. Test the vegetables by piercing with a knife. Cover with foil if the potatoes are browning too quickly. Once cooked, finish, if necessary, under a hot grill for that golden colour.

Variations

For a creamier texture, sit the dish in a roasting tray filled with hot water to come three-quarters of the way up the dish, cover with foil and bake in the oven for 1–1¼ hours, finishing under the grill.

This dish eats well without the celeriac as a straightforward Dauphinoise Potato. I also like to run anchovy fillets through the centre of the potatoes to add another taste.

Boulangère Potatoes

This is another potato dish with the potatoes simply sliced with onions and cooked in the oven in stock. It is a classic French recipe that is served in restaurants all over Britain, traditionally with roast best ends or legs of lamb.

SERVES 4

25–50 g (1–2 oz) unsalted butter
2 onions, sliced
675 g (1½ lb) potatoes, thinly sliced
Salt and freshly ground white pepper

450 ml (15 fl oz) Chicken Stock (see p.222) or Vegetable Stock (see p.223), warm

Pre-heat the oven to 230°C/450°F/gas 8.

Melt a little of the butter and fry the onions until softened. Reserve some good round potato slices to arrange on the top of the dish, then mix the remainder with the cooked onions and season with salt and pepper. Place the mixture in an ovenproof vegetable dish and cover with the reserved potato slices, overlapping them across the top. Pour over the warm stock and dot with the remaining butter. Cook in the pre-heated oven for 20 minutes until the potatoes begin to colour. Reduce the oven temperature to 200°C/400°F/gas 6 and cook for a further 40–50 minutes, pressing down the potatoes with a spatula occasionally for more even cooking. By the end of cooking, the potatoes will have absorbed the stock and should be golden and crispy on top. To finish, just sit the potatoes under the grill to achieve that extra rich colour.

Variations

There are a good many variations you can try. Add some strips of smoked bacon; sliced leeks; truffles (very nice – expensive, too!); sliced celeriac; sage and thyme – or just use your imagination!

Beetroot Fritters

These fritters eat very well with a classic accompaniment of just salt and vinegar, and also eat well if just dipped in soured cream or yoghurt and chives. They make a good alternative vegetable dish or can be used as a vegetarian starter (using the right beer).

To cook beetroot, plunge it into boiling salted water then return to the boil. The cooking time depends on age and size. Don't test them with a fork or they will bleed. Lift one out of the water after 30 minutes and try to pull back the skin with your thumb. If the skin comes off easily, the beetroot is cooked. If not, continue to test every 5–10 minutes. Once cooked, drain and leave to cool, then peel, cut in half and cut into 2 cm (¾ in) wedges. You can serve them as they are with some salad dressing or vinegar, sugar and a little water mixed together and poured over, or you can try this!

SERVES 4

450 g (1 lb) self-raising flour	12 beetroot wedges
Salt	Salt and freshly ground black pepper
300 ml (10 fl oz) lager	Malt vinegar (optional)
Oil for deep-frying	

Mix the flour and salt into the lager until you have a smooth, thick batter with almost a glue-like consistency. Pre-heat a deep frying-pan to 180°C/350°F. Season the beetroot wedges and dust with flour. Coat with batter. Drop into the hot fat and fry for a few minutes until crisp and golden. Remove and salt lightly. Sprinkle with vinegar before serving, if liked.

Variations

Parsnips also work well in this recipe. Peel and quarter the parsnips lengthways, cut the root from the centre and blanch the parsnips in boiling salted water for 2–3 minutes. Drain, cool and pat dry. Lightly flour, coat with batter and cook in the same way, then salt lightly before serving.

Beetroot Fritters.

Beetroot Bubble and Squeak

Bubble and squeak is traditionally made using potatoes, onions and Brussels sprouts, the name coming from the noise it makes while cooking. I get the occasional mad idea of what variations can be made to the dish – here's one that actually works. It goes well with venison, pheasant, pigeon or just about any game. It also eats well with most meats, making a roast leg of pork or lamb, for example, just that bit more interesting. Top it with spinach and a crumble mix to make a complete vegetarian dish.

SERVES 4

2 large onions, sliced
50 g (2 oz) unsalted butter
225 g (8 oz) beetroot, cooked and grated
175 g (6 oz) Mashed Potatoes (see p.133), made without milk or cream

Salt and freshly ground white pepper
1 tablespoon plain flour

Cook the onions in half the butter for a few minutes until softened but not coloured. Leave to cool.

Mix the beetroot with the potatoes, add the onions and season with salt and pepper. Stir well. The mix will be a shocking pink colour. It can now be fried as one large cake (the classic bubble) or shaped into small cakes. Pre-heat a frying-pan. Dust the bubble cakes with a little flour and fry in the remaining butter over a medium heat for about 4–5 minutes until golden brown on each side.

Variations

This can become a black pudding and beetroot cake by dicing and frying some black pudding and bacon (or pieces of sausage) and adding it to the mix before frying it. Serve it with a fried egg on top and grilled tomatoes.

Try making potato and onion bubble, top it with slices of corned beef, then thick slices of tomato, season and dot with butter then pop under the grill. If you're feeling really mad, top the lot with slices of Cheddar and let it melt over the bubble!

Glazed Carrots

Cooking carrots has become a very standard job. While they are a useful everyday vegetable, they are great to flavour so many things and I like cooking them this way to make them really tasty and exciting to eat.

SERVES 4

450 g (1 lb) carrots
A pinch of salt
Water

1 teaspoon caster sugar
25–50 g (1–2 oz) unsalted butter
Salt and freshly ground black pepper

The carrots can just be sliced into rings for this recipe, but I like to split them lengthways, twice if they are thick, then cut them at an angle into 1 cm (½ in) pieces. This gives more substance and texture to the vegetable. Place the carrots in a pan with a pinch of salt. Literally just cover, and only just, with water. Add the sugar and butter. Bring the water to the boil, then simmer until the carrots are just tender but still with a slight bite. The cooking time will be determined by how you have sliced them; 8–15 minutes. Drain the liquor into another pan and boil to reduce until 5–6 tablespoons are left. In the reduction process, the butter and sugar content will thicken the liquor, giving you a glaze. Add a little more butter if you want to thicken it a little more. Add the carrots to the pan and re-heat in the glaze. This will give them a wonderful, appetizing shine. Check the seasoning and serve.

Green Beans and Runner Beans

Green beans, known as haricots verts *in the catering industry, must be the most popular vegetable in restaurants; what we consider a first-class vegetable. They need minimum preparation – just top and tail them – and cook quickly. You can even buy them ready trimmed in most supermarkets!*

Another advantage is that you can cook them hours in advance, refresh them in iced water, then re-heat them later when you are ready to eat.

The secret to keeping good colour on any green vegetable is to make sure the water is salted and boiling rapidly before you add the vegetables, don't use a lid, and don't cook too many at once. For home cooking, it's best to cook only 450 g (1 lb) at a time. This is plenty for four to six portions.

To cook beans or any green vegetables, have a large pan three-quarters full of boiling water with a good pinch of salt. Drop in the beans and return the water to the boil. If the beans are extra fine they will be just about cooked; if just fine, cook for 30–45 seconds once the water has re-boiled. Check the beans during cooking; they should always have a good bite in them. Drain the beans and toss them in a knob of butter, seasoning with salt and a good twist of pepper.

The exception to this method is spinach, which is best cooked from raw in melted butter. It will cook and create all its own juices.

Runner beans are another favourite. To prepare these, just top and tail them, pulling away the sinewy string on either side. Cut the beans at an angle into thin 5–7.5 cm (2–3 in) strips. This way, the beans are cooked as soon as the water returns to the boil. If you prefer large pieces, cut them into 2.5 cm (1 in) diamonds; these will take 1–2 minutes.

When cut into strips, runner beans leave lots of room for extra tastes. I like to mix them with sliced onions cooked until golden in butter with strips of smoked bacon.

A selection of fresh runner beans, green beans and carrots.

Fresh Peas

Fresh peas are lovely to eat, providing they are properly cooked. Remember, don't try to cook too many at once, and don't cover the pan.

Once the peas have been shelled, bring a large pan of salted water to the boil. Drop in the peas, return the water to the boil and boil for 15–20 minutes, keeping the water boiling all the time. If the peas are not tender by that time, just keep boiling until they are ready. Drain off the peas, toss in butter and season with salt and pepper. Peas also eat well mixed with Glazed Carrots (see p.141); this then becomes a Flemish-style dish. Of course, you could substitute frozen peas.

This is a classic French dish called petits pois à la française. *It is almost braised peas with onions and lettuce, with the liquor thickend with a little flour. Well, I've changed it slightly and this is what I do.*

SERVES 4

50 g (2 oz) unsalted butter
2 onions, sliced
4 rashers smoked streaky bacon, rinded and cut into strips

50–85 ml (2–3 fl oz) Chicken Stock (see p.222) or Vegetable Stock (see p.223)
Salt and freshly ground black pepper
450 g (1 lb) peas, cooked

Melt 25 g (1 oz) of butter and cook the onions and bacon until slightly softened. Add the stock and bring to the boil. Add the remaining butter and season with salt and pepper. Quickly re-heat the peas for 30 seconds in a pan of boiling water, then drain off. Toss the peas in the reduced bacon and onion liquor and serve.

Fried Spinach, Mushrooms and Beansprouts

This eats well on its own but is even better with the Seared Spicy Pork Belly (see p.100).

SERVES 4

750–900 g (1½–2 lb) spinach
1–2 tablespoons olive oil
25 g (1 oz) unsalted butter
225 g (8 oz) cup mushrooms, sliced

225 g (8 oz) beansprouts, blanched in hot water
Salt and freshly ground black pepper
Juice of 1 lime

First remove the stalks from the spinach and tear the leaves carefully into small pieces. Wash the leaves and leave to dry.

Heat a wok or frying-pan and add the olive oil and butter. Add the mushrooms and toss for 30 seconds. Add the beansprouts and continue to cook for 2 minutes. Add the spinach and continue to stir for 30 seconds. Add the seasoning and lime juice and cook for about 30 seconds more until the vegetables are just tender.

Braised Lentils

Braised lentils can be used in so many dishes – fish or meat – and is perfect as an accompaniment to a main course or as a vegetable dish in its own right.

Serves 4

50 g (2 oz) unsalted butter
1 carrot, finely diced
1 small onion, finely diced
2 celery sticks, finely diced
225 g (8 oz) lentils

1 piece of bacon trimming (optional)
900 ml (1½ pints) Vegetable Stock (see p.223) or Chicken Stock (see p.222)
Salt and freshly ground black pepper

Pre-heat the oven to 200°C/400°F/gas 6.

Melt the butter in a flameproof casserole and fry the finely diced vegetables for a few minutes. Add the lentils and bacon, if using, and fry for a further minute. Add about 600 ml (1 pint) of the stock, making sure the lentils are just covered with stock, and bring to a simmer. Cover with a lid and cook in the pre-heated oven for 30–40 minutes, stirring occasionally, until the lentils are tender. As the lentils cook, they will tenderize as they absorb the stock. You may need to add a little more stock during cooking.

You can serve the lentils straight away, or they can be cooled and chilled. They will keep in the fridge for two to three days and can be re-heated in a spoonful of stock or water with a knob of butter.

Variations

This recipe can also be made into lentil soup by doubling the quantity of stock. Bacon is a good flavouring for lentils, so try adding a small dice or piece of bacon during cooking. If you've had a boiled bacon collar dish for lunch or dinner one day, then make sure that you keep all the stock it cooked in and dice any left-over bacon. With some chopped vegetables, you'll have an almost instant lentil and bacon soup to put together.

Puddings

T his is a very full chapter: lots of puddings with lots of features, recipes for different kinds of biscuits, chocolate puddings, steamed sponges and, of course, a whole section of home-made ice-creams.

The ice-cream feature runs from a straight Vanilla Ice-cream to Honey and Whisky Ice-cream and even a Black Forest Arctic Roll!

ABOVE *Knickerbockerglory (see p.204).*
LEFT *Adding the honey to Griddled Honey Apples (see p.166).*

Ice-cream recipes could be endless. The ones I have included are all personal favourites that have simple alternative methods for those in a hurry. You could almost make them all using a bought vanilla ice-cream, then stirring in the other flavourings.

There's also some simple tart recipes, including Treacle Tart and one of my favourites from 'school dinner' days, Gypsy Tart.

Pineapple Fritters

This recipe uses the same cider batter I used for Apple Fritters in Rhodes Around Britain. *That's the beauty of cooking, so many flavours help each other. With these I like to serve Coconut Ice-cream (see p.195) and Rum Custard Sauce (see p.215). It's almost like eating a hot Piña Colada cocktail! The fritters also eat well with clotted cream and Chocolate Sauce (see p.216). If you don't fancy either of these serving ideas, just pour over fresh cream.*

SERVES 4

1 small, ripe pineapple
300 ml (10 fl oz) sweet cider
100 g (4 oz) plain flour plus a little extra
    for coating

25 g (1 oz) caster sugar
Vegetable oil for deep-frying

Cut the outside skin from the pineapple, then split it into quarters. Remove the central core from all four pieces. Each quarter can now be cut into three leaving you with twelve large chunks.

To make the batter, mix together the cider, flour and sugar. Heat the oil to about 180°C/350°F. Lightly flour the pineapple chunks, then dip them into the batter and deep-fry for about 5 minutes until crispy and golden. You may need to do this in batches.

Pineapple and Almond Tart

This tart eats really well sitting on a rich Chocolate Sauce (see p.216) and topped with Coconut Ice-cream (see p.195). All those flavours work so well with pineapple. The pineapple should be fresh and ripe. This will be a deep yellow colour with a moist sweet taste. If you find the pineapple to be firm and opaque in colour, the fruit will need to be poached in some Stock Syrup (see p.217) until tender. This dish can also be made using a good quality tinned pineapple. You can make this pudding with lots of different fruits from apple and blackberry to raspberry, pear or peach. All these fruits work with different ice-creams and sauces.

SERVES 6–8

225 g (8 oz) Shortcrust Pastry (see p.211)
½ fresh pineapple, peeled

2 tablespoons pineapple jam (optional)
1 quantity Almond Paste (see p.213)
Icing sugar, sifted

Pre-heat the oven to 190°C/375°F/gas 5 and grease a 25 cm (10 in) flan ring.

Roll out the pastry, use to line the flan ring and leave to rest in the fridge. Cut the pineapple into 2 cm (¾ in) cubes. For extra pineapple taste, spread some pineapple jam on to the pastry base first before spooning in the almond paste and smoothing over.

Push the pineapple cubes into the almond paste. During the cooking of this tart the almond paste will become liquid and flood the tart case. As the paste cooks it will develop a moist sponge texture. Bake the tart in the pre-heated oven. The tart will take between 45–60 minutes. The almond paste will rise slightly.

To give an extra finish and glaze to the tart, sprinkle liberally with icing sugar and glaze under the grill.

Note

For a different finish to the dish, liberally scatter diced fresh pineapple over the top of the tart 10 minutes before it is completely cooked and return it to the oven. The tart can still be finished with the icing sugar glazed under the grill, giving a slight burnt tinge to the pineapple.

Apricot and Almond Tart

For this recipe I'm using a large 28 cm (11 in) diameter x 4 cm (1½ in) deep flan ring which really does make a large pudding. The recipe can easily be cut down by half and a smaller 18 cm (7 in) flan ring can be used. You can use whichever stock syrup you prefer for this recipe.

The flan eats well hot or cold and goes well with clotted cream, custard or ice-cream and is a great alternative for Christmas when served with Christmas Pudding Ice-cream (see p.194).

SERVES 6–8

20 dried, ready-soaked stoned apricots	4 tablespoons apricot jam
300 ml (10 fl oz) Stock Syrup (see p.217)	1 quantity Almond Paste (see p.213)
225 g (8 oz) Shortcrust Pastry (see p.211)	Icing sugar, sifted

Pre-heat the oven to 190°C/375°F/gas 5. Butter and lightly flour a 28 cm (11 in) flan ring.

Split the apricots through the middle, leaving circular discs of fruit. Warm the stock syrup with the fruits and then leave to cool. These can be prepared and chilled days in advance or left until the last minute and drained off before using. The stock will still keep in the fridge. This process softens the apricots even more and leaves them tender.

Roll out the pastry and use to line the flan case. Heat the jam and reduce by half. Spread the jam over the pastry base, then place 20 apricot pieces evenly over the jam. Spoon over the almond paste, leaving a smooth finish on top, and filling to about three-quarters of the way up to allow for it to rise during cooking. Bake in the pre-heated oven for 45 minutes. Remove from the oven and arrange the remaining apricots on top in a circular pattern. (If you put them on before cooking, they sink into the almond paste as it warms and loosens.) Return to the oven for a further 10–20 minutes until golden brown and just firming to the touch.

Sprinkle the flan liberally with icing sugar and glaze under a hot grill, allowing the sugar to caramelize and almost burn in places for a bitter sweet taste.

Apricot and Almond Tart.

Chocolate and Pear Brûlée

Chocolate and pears are a classic combination; the flavours work so well together. The texture of the brûlée has an almost chocolate-toffee consistency which can become more toffee-ish if you use extra chocolate.

I like to eat crème brûlées at room temperature so the consistency is similar to egg custard. However, this pudding can also be eaten chilled.

SERVES 4

8 egg yolks
50 g (2 oz) caster sugar
600 ml (1 pint) double cream
100 g (4 oz) or more good quality plain
   chocolate, grated

4–6 Poached Pear halves (see p.181) or
   tinned pear halves
100 g (4 oz) icing sugar, sifted

Pre-heat the oven to 160–180°C/325–350°F/gas 3–4.

Beat the egg yolks and sugar together in a bowl. Bring the cream to the boil and whisk it into the egg yolk mix. Sit the bowl over a pan of hot water and heat until the custard thickens, stirring all the time; it should have the consistency of double cream. Add the grated chocolate and stir until melted. The mix should now be tasted. If the chocolate flavour is not strong enough, simply keep adding, stirring and tasting until you have the right flavour. Divide the chocolate custard between individual ramekins and sit them in a roasting tray. Fill the tray with hot water to come three-quarters up the sides of the moulds. Finish in the pre-heated oven for 20–30 minutes until the mix thickens and sets. Check the brûlées by removing a ramekin from the tray and shaking gently. The brûlée should be only slightly runny in the centre. If the mix is still too liquid, return to the oven and check after a further 5 minutes. Once cooked, remove from the oven and tray and allow to cool to room temperature.

To finish the dish, cut the pears lengthways into slices and arrange overlapping on top of each pudding. Sprinkle liberally with icing sugar and glaze under a hot grill until you have a golden crisp sugar topping. To achieve a good glaze the icing sugar may have to be applied two or three times.

Variations

It's also possible to slice a quarter of a pear per pudding, then dice the remaining fruit and place it in the bottom of the ramekins before adding the brûlée.

Steamed Sponge Pudding

These puddings are real homely classics – just the sort of pudding to finish your meal, especially for a Sunday lunch. Steamed sponges seem to be playing a big part in The Great British Revival. In fact, steamed lemon sponge was one of the, if not the, first pudding that I made. The sponge can be so light and fluffy to eat and will take on so many other flavours, many of which I am featuring here.

To make it a lot easier to turn out the puddings, use plastic moulds which hold up very well to steaming, and when lightly pressed the sponge should fall out easily. You can use 150 ml (5 fl oz) individual moulds or a 900 ml (1½ pint) mould.

SERVES 4–6

100 g (4 oz) unsalted butter
150 g (5 oz) caster sugar
2 eggs
1 egg yolk
200 g (7 oz) self-raising flour

1–2 drops of milk, if needed
Lightly butter and flour 4 × 150 ml
(5 fl oz) moulds or one 900 ml
(1½ pint) pudding basin.

Beat the butter and sugar together until almost white in colour and the sugar has dissolved. This is easily achieved in an electric mixer. It does, however, take a little while to cream to this stage. Beat in one egg at a time, making sure after each egg is added that the mix is beaten until completely mixed and fluffy again. Once both eggs have been added, continue with the same process for the egg yolk. Most recipes will tell you now to fold in the flour slowly and carefully. Well, I want you to do almost the opposite. Add the flour and beat until all the flour has completely creamed into the mix but do not over-work. Add the milk if needed.

Spoon in the mixture, filling each mould one three-quarters full. Cover the moulds with lightly buttered squares of tin foil, just lightly folding the foil over the rims so the sponge can rise and push up the foil during cooking. Steam the sponges over boiling water, allowing 35–40 minutes for individual puddings or 1¼ – 1½ hours for the larger mould. Top up the boiling water as necessary during cooking.

Golden Syrup Sponge

Golden syrup sponge is always a favourite - just add a generous spoon of syrup to the sponge mixture and sit some more in the base of each mould and then steam. Pour a little more syrup on top before serving (see overleaf).

Steamed Lemon Sponge with Lemon Curd Ice-cream and Lemon Custard Sauce

This sponge eats beautifully with lemon curd ice-cream and lemon custard sauce (see preceding pages). If you feel this is all a bit too strong, simply serve the pudding with one or the other and some whipped or pouring double cream.

SERVES 4–6

1 Steamed Sponge Pudding recipe (see p.153)
Finely grated zest of 1 lemon
Juice of 1 lemon

A little milk
Lemon Curd Ice-cream (see p.197)
Lemon Custard Sauce (see p.215)

Add the lemon zest to the butter and sugar mixture in the basic sponge method, then continue to make the sponge until the flour has been added and mixed. Fold in the lemon juice and a little milk, if necessary. Because the zest was in at the beginning the flavour will become more powerful and strong. The sponges can now be steamed in the usual way (see p.153).

PRECEDING PAGES *Clockwise, starting top left:*
Steamed Chocolate Sponge (see p.160); Golden Syrup Sponge (see p.153);
Steamed Lemon Sponge with Lemon Curd Ice-cream
and Lemon Custard Sauce (see above);
Steamed Apricot Sponge with Apricot Sauce (see p.159);
and Steamed Orange Sponge with Hot Orange Sauce
and Marmalade Ice-cream (see p.158).

Steamed Lemon and Rhubarb Sponge

Using the redcurrant jelly with the rhubarb is an optional extra that helps enrich the liquor and juices from the sugared rhubarb. If eaten cold, the mixture will almost set to jam. The beauty of the recipe is that so many other flavours work with it. A little ginger may be added, or you can use other fruits such as blackberries or blueberries. The rhubarb recipe can also be cooked a little more and then puréed and turned into a sorbet or ice-cream (see p.189).

You can make individual puddings or one large one. The flavours of the rhubarb and lemon work really well together, and you can serve the dessert with pouring cream, Lemon Custard (see p.215) or even Vanilla Ice-cream (see p.190).

SERVES 4–6

450 g (1 lb) fresh rhubarb	1 tablespoon of redcurrant jelly
25 g (1 oz) unsalted butter	(optional)
225 g (8 oz) caster sugar	1 Steamed Lemon Sponge (see p.156)

Peel any coarse skin from the rhubarb stalks; young, tender rhubarb will not need to be peeled. Cut the rhubarb into 2 cm (¾ in) pieces. Melt the butter in a pan until it begins to bubble. Add the rhubarb and stir gently for 1–2 minutes. Add the sugar and bring to the simmer. As the rhubarb is warming it will also be cooking. When it becomes tender, after about 4–5 minutes depending on size and ripeness, remove from the heat. Stir in the redcurrant jelly, if using. Allow the rhubarb mix to cool.

Butter and flour one large mould or individual moulds. Spoon 4–5 tablespoons of the rhubarb into the large mould or 1 tablespoon into the individual moulds, cover with the lemon sponge mix and finish and cook in the usual way (see page 153).

When the sponges are cooked, re-heat the remaining rhubarb. Turn out the puddings and spoon some more fruit over the top.

Steamed Orange Sponge with Hot Orange Sauce and Marmalade Ice-cream

This pudding gives us three different orange flavours from bitter to sweet, and also three different textures (see pp.154–55). It has to be my favourite steamed sponge. The whole dish is packed with orange flavour.

Serves 4–6

100 g (4 oz) unsalted butter
150 g (5 oz) caster sugar
2 eggs
1 egg yolk

Finely grated zest of 1 orange
200 g (7 oz) self-raising flour
Juice of 2–3 oranges, boiled to reduce by two-thirds then cooled

For the Sauce

600 ml (1 pint) fresh orange juice
25–50 g (1–2 oz) caster sugar
1 teaspoon arrowroot or cornflour
1 tablespoon cold water

Marmalade Ice-cream to serve (see p.198)
A few fresh mint sprigs

To make the sponge, cream the butter and sugar together. Mix the eggs and egg yolk together and beat into the butter and sugar mix. Add the orange zest and fold in the flour. Add the orange juice, making sure it is cold.

Line six 150 ml (5 fl oz) moulds or one 900 ml (1½ pint) mould with butter and flour. Spoon in the sponge mix to fill three-quarters of the way up the mould and cover with buttered paper or tin foil. Steam individual puddings for about 35-40 minutes or larger puddings for 1¼–1½ hours.

Meanwhile, make the orange sauce. Boil the orange juice until reduced by half, then add the sugar to taste (start with a tablespoon and add until you have the sweetness you want). Mix the arrowroot or cornflour with the water then whisk a few drops at a time into the simmering juice until you have a good sauce/coating consistency. Allow to cook for 3–4 minutes.

Once the pudding is cooked, just turn out and serve with a spoonful of marmalade ice-cream, some hot orange sauce and a sprig of mint.

Variations

This is a recipe for a basic orange sauce. To change the flavour, some grated zest can be added or a little Cointreau, Grand Marnier or brandy can be added to lift the taste.

Steamed Apricot Sponge with Apricot Sauce

This recipe has many alternatives – you can use dried or tinned apricots, or even apricot jam. This, of course, makes it quite a rich pudding that is packed with flavour.

When buying dried apricots it's best to select 'ready-to-eat' or no-soak ones that are available in almost all supermarkets. They still have about 25 per cent moisture left in them, which leaves them soft and almost toffee-like to eat straight from the packet. Also for this recipe choose the apricots which are still orange in colour. The texture of this dish is lovely to eat. You have good soft apricots on top of a light fluffy sponge with the rich sauce. The best accompaniment is simply clotted cream and apricot sauce.

SERVES 4–6

12–16 ready-to-eat dried apricots
1 × 425 g (15 oz) tin halved apricots in syrup
1 Steamed Sponge Pudding recipe (see p.153)

1 tablespoon apricot jam
Icing sugar, sifted

It's best to start this recipe either in the morning or day before to achieve the best flavour from the apricots. To give them more moisture and flavour they should be soaked in some syrup, and with this recipe you don't even have to make it. Just open the tinned apricots and pour off and keep the syrup. Warm the syrup and add the dried apricots. Leave them to stand for a few hours. The apricots should be a little softer and more juicy.

Grease and flour six 150 ml (5 fl oz) moulds or one 900 ml (1½ pint) mould.

You can now place three halves of apricot per portion, without syrup, into the bottom of the individual or large pudding moulds. If you have soaked some extra, then simply chop them up and mix into the basic sponge mix. Spoon the mix on top and steam as for the basic recipe (see p.153).

To make the apricot sauce, blend the tinned apricots to a purée. Warm in a pan with the apricot jam, then add enough of the remaining syrup until you have a good sauce consistency. The sauce may taste a little sharp. To help this, just add some icing sugar a pinch at a time until you have the right sweetness. Push the sauce through a sieve and it is ready.

Once the sponge is cooked, turn out on to a plate and spoon the warm sauce over.

Steamed Chocolate Sponge

Along with steamed jam sponge, this has to be a children's favourite. In fact, I think it's a favourite for everyone (see pp.154–55). One of the pleasures of cooking is never allowing recipes to be over-strict. This pudding can have so many different textures and tastes added from walnuts and almonds to dates and orange zest – and many more.

There are two or three sauces which go very well with this pudding. Try Chocolate Sauce (see p.216), Coffee Custard Sauce (see p.215) or Pecan Nut Sauce (see p.168). It's all very rich but very tasty!

SERVES 4–6

1 Steamed Sponge Pudding recipe (see p.153), omitting 50 g (2 oz) of the self-raising flour	50 g (2 oz) cocoa 50–100 g (2–4 oz) good quality plain chocolate, grated

Simply follow the basic sponge recipe mixing the cocoa with remaining self-raising flour. Stir the grated chocolate into the mix to lift the flavour and texture.

To cook this pudding, only steam for 35 minutes if using individual moulds or for 1½ hours in a large mould. This leaves it slightly softer in the centre. Turn out and serve with the sauce of your choice. I also like to finish the dish with either grated chocolate or chocolate shavings.

Cloutie Dumpling

I ate this recipe for pudding when I visited Alan Craigie at the Creel Restaurant in the Orkneys while filming Rhodes Around Britain. *It was delicious. What did surprise me was that I had also eaten it that morning with my cooked breakfast! Now that's what I call variety.*

Cloutie dumpling is a Scottish speciality. Cloutie comes from the word 'clout' meaning cloth, which is what the dumpling is wrapped in before boiling. I would describe it as a light Christmas dumpling. For me, it ate best as a pudding with lots of thick cream.

If you have any left over, just cut it into slices and shallow fry in butter for breakfast the next day.

SERVES 4–6

175 g (6 oz) self-raising flour
175 g (6 oz) brown breadcrumbs
175 g (6 oz) shredded suet
100 g (4 oz) currants
175 g (6 oz) raisins
175 g (6 oz) sultanas
1 teaspoon bicarbonate of soda

A good pinch of ground ginger
A good pinch of freshly grated nutmeg
A good pinch of ground cinnamon
100 g (4 oz) soft dark brown sugar
2 tablespoons golden syrup or treacle
250 ml (8 fl oz) milk

Simply mix all the ingredients together. Boil a large cloth then dust with flour. Place the mix in the cloth, then pull the cloth around, making a ball shape. Boil in a pan of water for 2–2½ hours, topping up as necessary, then unwrap, slice and serve with cream.

Blackberry Jam Tart

I used to love jam tarts as a child: just sweet pastry tartlet moulds filled with jam. I thought they were really delicious. Well, this recipe is for a jam tart with a difference. I have always felt that a jam tart needed another texture, so read on and you'll see exactly what I mean!

For this recipe I'm going to use four individual tartlet cases, but a 28 cm (11 in) flan case will be fine. If you use a large flan case, the pastry can be left raw before adding the almond mix then all baked at the same time, in which case it will need 1–1¼ hours.

The jam tart eats well just with thick or clotted cream. I also like to serve home-made Custard Sauce (see p.215) either cold or warm, or sometimes flavoured with calvados.

SERVES 4–6

175–225 g (6–8 oz) Puff Pastry (see p.212)	175 g (6 oz) ground almonds
175 g (6 oz) unsalted butter	40 g (1½ oz) plain flour
175 g (6 oz) caster sugar	3 eggs, size 2
	225 g (8 oz) Blackberry Jam (see p.210)

Pre-heat the oven to 180°C/350°F/gas 4.

Roll out the pastry thinly and line the flan cases, leaving any excess pastry hanging over the edge of the rings. This will prevent the pastry from shrinking back into the mould during baking. Leave to rest for 20 minutes. Line the pastry with greaseproof paper and fill with baking beans or rice and bake in the pre-heated oven for 15–20 minutes until the pastry is cooked and set. Remove the paper and beans and cut off any excess pastry hanging over the flan cases. To do this, simply take a sharp knife, position it at the top of the tart ring and cut all the pastry away. By cutting this way the pastry will be neatly flush with the tart case.

You can, of course, make the filling in a food mixer or processor. Beat the butter and sugar together until well creamed. Fold in the almonds and flour. Beat in one egg at a time, making sure they are well mixed in. Spoon the almond filling into the flan case, leaving it about 2 mm from the top. (If you find you have some mix left over, then simply chill it and it will keep for up to one week.) Bake the tarts in the pre-heated oven, allowing 30–35 minutes for the small tarts or 45–60 minutes for a large flan case. When cooked, the tarts will be firm to the touch and a knife inserted in the centre will come out almost clean.

Once cooked the almond sponge mix should have risen slightly. This can simply be sliced off the top to expose the sponge. While the tart is still warm, spoon some of the jam over the tarts until just covered. Return to the oven for 1–2 minutes by which time the jam will be making its way through the sponge. To serve, simply remove the flan case and eat either hot or cold.

Variations

We all know what a great combination blackberry and apple is. If you really want to make this different and give other tastes then simply add some grated apple to the almond mix, or place poached apples or pears in the pastry cases before spooning on the mix. This gives you different textures as well as tastes.

Treacle Tart

This is a very quick and easy recipe. It has, like so many other recipes, many alternatives. Half a teaspoon of ground ginger works very well, so does the addition of a little grated orange zest, or you can enrich the whole recipe with the addition of a few tablespoons of double cream and one or two eggs. You can eat it on its own or with clotted or pouring cream.

SERVES 4

1 quantity Sweet Pastry (see p.211)
50 g (2 oz) unsalted butter
10 tablespoons golden syrup

225 g (8 oz) fresh breadcrumbs
Finely grated zest and juice of 1 lemon

Pre-heat the oven to 200°C/400°F/gas 6.

Roll out the pastry and use to line a 23 cm (9 in) flan ring. Cover with greaseproof paper and baking beans or rice and bake in the pre-heated oven for 10–15 minutes until set. Remove the paper and beans. Reduce the oven temperature to 180°C/350°F/gas 4.

Melt the butter and syrup together. Add the breadcrumbs and lemon juice and zest. Pour the mix into the pastry case and bake in the oven for 20 minutes. If the treacle filling is bubbling, then remove from the oven. If it is not quite at that stage, cook for a further 5–10 minutes. When the treacle is at the bubbling/sizzling stage, remove the tart from the oven and allow to settle. The tart can be eaten warm or cold.

Gypsy Tart

This is a recipe I had been searching for for years. It's a pudding I remember from school days and it was my favourite. When I found somebody who knew the dish and was given the recipe I couldn't believe how simple it is – and it still tastes great.

SERVES 6

225 g (8 oz) Shortcrust Pastry
   (see p.211)

1 × 400 g (14 oz) tin evaporated milk
350 g (12 oz) dark muscovado sugar

Pre-heat the oven to 200°C/400°F/gas 6.

Roll out the pastry and use to line a 25 cm (10 in) flan ring. Line with greaseproof paper and baking beans and bake in the pre-heated oven for 15–20 minutes until cooked. Leave to cool.

Whisk the evaporated milk and sugar together for 10–15 minutes until light and fluffy. The mix should be coffee coloured. Pour the mix into the pastry case and bake in the oven for 10 minutes. The gypsy tart will now have a slightly sticky surface but will not set completely until it has been left to cool. Serve cold. I told you this recipe was easy!

Toffee

This really is amazing. When I show people the results, most just can't believe it. As you can see you don't need a lot of ingredients! The toffee is great for so many things: crumbles, creams, ice-creams and sauces. You'll find some of the recipes in the book.

MAKES 400 g (14 oz)

1 × 400 g (14 oz) tin condensed milk

All you have to do is place the tin of condensed milk (totally unopened) into a pan and cover with cold water, making sure the tin is completely covered. Bring to the boil and continue to simmer for 3 hours (no less!). Leave to cool down in the pan. The toffee is now made and can be kept chilled in the unopened can until the date runs out.

Toffee Cream

The standard proportions for this recipe are one tin of Toffee to 450 ml (15 fl oz) of cream, but this makes a lot of cream, so it is best to make it in a smaller quantity.

SERVES 4

200 g (7 oz) Toffee (see p.164)   250 ml (8 fl oz) double or single cream

Stir the toffee in a bowl to loosen. If you're looking for a thick pouring cream, then simply add all the cream and whisk in until well mixed (single cream works well for this). If you want a thick and light cream, then use double cream, just adding a quarter of the cream and whisking until thickened, then adding another quarter, and so on until everything is mixed. The toffee cream may still seem to be a little soft, so it's best to make this 1–2 hours before you need it and then chill it in the fridge. This will give the cream a totally new texture and, when spooned on to the plate, it will hold its shape.

Griddled Honey Apples with Toffee Cream

This must be the easiest and quickest apple pudding there is, so if you're ever stuck and time is running out, have a go! It's great to eat with the toffee cream but also works really well with just pouring cream or Vanilla Ice-cream (see p.190).

To speed up the glazing of the top, I use a gas gun, which works really well to caramelize sugar. However, please don't use one of these unless you're very familiar with them.

SERVES 2

3 apples, peeled and cored
15 g (½ oz) unsalted butter
4 teaspoons clear honey

2–3 tablespoons icing sugar, sifted
Toffee Cream (see p.165) to serve
2 sprigs of fresh mint (optional)

Slice the apples across through the middle to give six thick apple rings in total. Warm a frying-pan and add the butter. Sit the apples middle-side down into the pan and fry until the apples become a rich brown with tinges of burnt around the edges to give a bitter-sweet apple taste. Turn the apples and continue to cook over a medium heat for 1–2 minutes (or you can place them in a medium oven for 1–2 minutes until the apples become just tender).

Spoon the honey on top of the apples. Spoon the icing sugar into a teastrainer and sprinkle well over the top. Finish under a hot grill until the sugar becomes crispy. To increase the crunchy topping, just sprinkle more icing sugar on top and re-glaze.

To serve the apples, sit three pieces on to each plate and serve with thick toffee cream and a sprig of mint.

Griddled Honey Apples with Toffee Cream.

Chocolate Fudge Cake with Pecan Nut Sauce

This pudding is rich, sticky and very tasty. You won't be able to eat it too often but every now and again it's a wonderful treat. This makes quite a large cake but it is worth the effort. It keeps brilliantly for days in the fridge and can be simply microwaved a portion at a time or as a whole pudding. To serve the pudding just pour the pecan sauce over each slice.

SERVES 8

6 eggs	225 g (8 oz) unsalted butter
350 g (12 oz) caster sugar	100 g (4 oz) ground almonds
A few drops vanilla essence	150 g (5 oz) fresh white breadcrumbs
225 g (8 oz) good quality plain chocolate	

For the Pecan Nut Sauce

175 g (6 oz) soft brown sugar	85 ml (3 fl oz) double cream
100 g (4 oz) unsalted butter	25–50 g (1–2 oz) pecan nuts, chopped

Pre-heat the oven to 180°C/350°C/gas 4 and grease a 20 × 25 cm (8 × 10 in) baking tray. The baking tray needs to be at least 2.5 cm (1 in) deep to achieve the right texture.

Whisk together the eggs, sugar and vanilla essence until the mixture forms stiff peaks (sabayon stage). Melt the chocolate with the butter in a bowl over warm water. Pour on to the egg and sugar mixture and then fold in the ground almonds and breadcrumbs. The mix will be very loose, almost liquid. Pour the mix into the prepared baking tray and bake in the pre-heated oven for 50–60 minutes. The texture of the pudding should be cooked but almost stodgy and moist. The pudding should be left to rest for 10 minutes before serving.

To make the sauce, place the sugar, butter and cream in a saucepan and bring to the boil. Simmer the sauce until the sugar has dissolved. Stir in the pecan nuts. The sauce is now ready.

Chocolate Mousse

This is a rich and light chocolate mousse which can be served in glasses or moulds. It can also be layered between chocolate sponge (see p.160) in a terrine mould or round cake tin.

SERVES 8

150 g (5 oz) good quality plain chocolate
275 g (10 oz) unsalted butter, diced
150 g (5 oz) cocoa

300 ml (10 fl oz) double cream
200 g (7 oz) caster sugar
6 eggs, separated

Chop the chocolate and melt it slowly in a bowl over a pan of hot water. Add the butter and let it melt in the warmth of the chocolate. Add the cocoa and whisk in until the mix is smooth. Whisk the double cream until it forms soft peaks, then reserve in the fridge. Whisk half the sugar with all the yolks until pale and fluffy. Whisk the remaining sugar and egg whites together until they form stiff peaks.

Fold the chocolate mix with the egg yolks and sugar, add the meringue mix and lastly fold in the cream. The mousse can now be set in glasses or moulds and needs half a day minimum to set.

Variations

If you wish to make this into a chocolate mousse cake or terrine, simply cut the sponge to fit the mould, layer it with the mousse and set in the fridge. The sponge can now be finished with the chocolate coating recipe on page 172 to make a really spectacular cake.

Irish Chocolate Coffee Cake

This recipe was given to me by a close friend, Gabrielle, who produces Rhodes Around Britain. *We often have different ideas about cooking and filming, but one thing is for sure, we both want the same results, and with this dish she won. It eats and keeps beautifully, especially when flavoured with good Irish whiskey!*

MAKES 1 × 20 cm (8 in) cake

175 g (6 oz) good quality plain chocolate
4–6 tablespoons strong black coffee
2–4 tablespoons Irish whiskey
75 g (3 oz) caster sugar
100 g (4 oz) unsalted butter at room
    temperature

3 eggs, separated
A pinch of salt
50 g (2 oz) ground almonds
A few drops of almond essence
50 g (2 oz) plain flour, sifted

For the Icing

100 g (4 oz) good quality plain chocolate
2 tablespoons whiskey or strong coffee

100 g (4 oz) unsalted butter

Pre-heat the oven to 180°C/350°F/gas 4. Butter and flour a 20 cm (8 in) cake dish.

Melt the chocolate, coffee and whiskey in a bowl over a pan of simmering water, then cool to room temperature. Reserve a tablespoon of sugar, then cream together the remaining sugar with the butter until you have a pale yellow, fluffy mixture. Beat in the egg yolks until well blended. Whisk the egg whites and salt until soft peaks form. Sprinkle on the tablespoon of caster sugar and beat until stiff peaks form. With a rubber spatula, blend the melted chocolate into the butter and sugar mixture, then stir in the ground almonds and essence. Fold in a quarter of the egg whites, sift in a quarter of the flour, then continue folding and sifting alternately until everything is blended. Turn the mixture into the prepared cake dish, pushing the mixture up to the rim with the spatula. Bake in middle of the pre-heated oven for about 25–30 minutes. The cake is done when it has puffed, and a skewer pushed into the middle comes out clean. Allow the cake to cool. It must be thoroughly cold to be iced.

To make the icing, melt the chocolate and whiskey or coffee in a bowl over a pan of simmering water until you have a smooth cream. Remove the bowl from the heat and beat in the butter a tablespoon at a time. Stand the bowl over cold water and beat until the chocolate mixture is cool and of spreading consistency. Spread it over the cake and serve with Cheesecake Cream (see p.180).

Irish Chocolate Coffee Cake.with Cheesecake Cream (see p.180).

Chocolate Terrine

This is the sort of pudding for a special dinner party. It's rich in texture and taste and eats like a chocolate dream. One of the big advantages of making this dish is that it freezes so well and doesn't spoil. So if you've got a party coming up, make this now and just pop it in the freezer ready for the big day. The best size terrine mould to use is a Le Creuset 29 x 9 cm (11½ x 3½ in). The terrine mould is lined with a chocolate sponge, filled with a chocolate mousse and then coated with more chocolate.

SERVES 12

For the Sponge

225 g (8 oz) caster sugar
5 eggs, separated

100 g (4 oz) cocoa

For the Mousse

150 g (6 oz) good quality plain chocolate
175 g (6 oz) unsalted butter
75 g (3 oz) cocoa

300 ml (10 fl oz) double cream
4 eggs, separated
175 g (6 oz) caster sugar

For the Chocolate Coating

120 ml (4 fl oz) milk
65 ml (2½ fl oz) double cream

275 g (10 oz) good quality plain
    chocolate, chopped
65 g (2½ oz) unsalted butter, chopped

Pre-heat the oven to 160°C/325°F/gas 3 and butter and line a 40 × 30 cm (16 × 12 in) baking tray. Line a 29 × 9 cm (11½ × 3½ in) terrine with greaseproof paper or cling film.

To make the sponge, mix half the sugar with the egg yolks and whisk until pale and fluffy. Whisk the egg whites until they form soft peaks, then add the remaining sugar and continue to whisk to a stiff meringue. Fold the cocoa into the egg yolk mix, then whisk in a quarter of the meringue mix. Carefully and lightly fold in the remaining meringue. Spread the mix in the prepared tin. Bake in the pre-heated oven for about 20–30 minutes. Leave to cool.

To make the mousse, melt the chocolate with the butter in a bowl over a pan of warm water until it binds to a thick cream consistency. Add the cocoa and beat until completely smooth and cooled. Whisk the cream until it forms soft peaks, then chill. Whisk the egg yolks with half the sugar until white and fluffy. Fold into the chocolate mix. Whisk the egg whites with the remaining sugar to meringue stage, then fold into the chocolate mix. Now fold in the whipped cream.

Cut the cold sponge into four, making sure you measure from the mould, then line the base and sides, saving one piece for the top. Pour the chocolate mousse into the mould, then place the remaining piece of sponge on top. Chill for for 2–3 hours or freeze.

The chocolate coating finishes and really lifts the pudding. Bring the milk and cream to the boil, then pour on to the chocolate and butter. Stir until melted and blended. Cool until thick and at room temperature. To cover the terrine, remove from the fridge or freezer, spoon some on top and spread on until completely covered. Return to the fridge or freezer until set.

To finish, turn out the terrine on to a small board or tray, then spoon over the remaining chocolate coating and spread evenly over the sponge. The terrine will, of course, no longer fit in the mould and so can be kept chilled or frozen on the tray or board. Once the coating has completely set, just cover with cling film.

The terrine will make at least 12 portions. However, the finished dish can be cut into 4 and then frozen so that it can be eaten whenever you like.

Variations

This pudding can be made a lot easier by simply sitting half the sponge into a lined flan case and then pouring the mousse on top and finishing with another layer of sponge. This can then be set in a fridge or freezer. Remove the flan ring and lining and finish with the chocolate coating. It will look like a rich chocolate cake but is in fact a rich chocolate mousse.

This chocolate pudding eats very well with either Orange Custard Sauce (see p.215) or Coffee Custard Sauce (see p.215).

OVERLEAF *Clockwise, starting from the left:*
Basic Tuile Biscuits (see p.176); Gingerbread Biscuits (see p.179);
Brandy Snap Biscuits (see p.176); Chocolate Brownies (see p.178);
and Shortbread Biscuits (see p.177).

Basic Tuile Biscuits

This is a very basic tuile biscuit recipe (see preceding pages). They eat very well with ice-creams and make good baskets to sit the ice-cream in. This mix keeps for up to a week if kept chilled. You can also change the flavour by adding the finely grated zest of 1 lemon or 1 orange (or both) or a little desiccated coconut.

SERVES 4

120 g (4½ oz) unsalted butter	3 egg whites
150 g (5 oz) icing sugar, sifted	120 g (4½ oz) plain flour

Soften the butter and add the icing sugar, beating until white. Add the egg whites and fold in the flour. The mix is ready and should now be chilled to set.

Pre-heat the oven to 180°C/350°F/gas 4 and butter a baking sheet.

Spread the mix very thinly into 13 cm (5 in) discs. This can be made easy by cutting a 13 cm (5 in) circle from a thin plastic ice-cream tub lid, then just placing it on the tray and spreading the mix in, keeping level with the lid. Bake the tuiles in the pre-heated oven for 5–6 minutes until totally golden brown. Remove from the tray while still hot and place over a tin can or mould to shape the basket.

Variations

If you wish to serve these as biscuits to go with your coffee or serve separately with ice-creams, then simply make 6 cm (2½ in) discs and bake them the same way. To shape them, take the centre roll from cling film or tin foil and cut it lengthways to give two semi-circular halves. Sit the warm biscuits into the mould to set.

Brandy Snap Biscuits

Brandy snap biscuits are easy to make and can be made into various shapes and sizes (see preceding pages). I like to serve them with sorbets and ice-creams. If you roll this mix into balls the size of a 2p piece and push them on to a buttered tray, the mix will spread to give you a disc big enough to place over or in a cup to make a basket for your ice-creams. But always make sure that you keep a good distance between each one on the tray or you'll have just one large tray of brandy snap!

MAKES about 24

100 g (4 oz) unsalted butter	100 g (4 oz) plain flour
100 g (4 oz) caster sugar	A pinch of ground ginger
100 g (4 oz) golden syrup	A pinch of ground cinnamon

Place the butter, sugar and syrup in a pan and heat gently to dissolve. Remove from heat. Mix the flour with the ginger and cinnamon, then beat into the sugar mixture. Leave to cool.

Pre-heat the oven to 180°C/350°F/gas 4 and grease two baking sheets.

Roll the mixture into balls the size of a 2p piece and place well spaced out on the prepared trays. Bake in the pre-heated oven for 7–10 minutes until golden brown with a perforated texture. Leave to cool slightly for a minute before removing from the tray and moulding over a tea cup or round the handle of a wooden spoon. If the snaps cool before you can finish shaping them all, just pop them back in the oven to warm slightly.

Shortbread Biscuits

This recipe works best if piped on to a greased baking tray.

MAKES about 16

225 g (8 oz) unsalted butter	450 g (1 lb) plain flour
75 g (3 oz) caster sugar	15 g (½ oz) cornflour

Pre-heat the oven to 180°C/350°F/gas 4 and grease and line a baking sheet.

Cream together the butter and sugar until the sugar has dissolved into the fat. Sift the flour and cornflour together and work into the butter mix. Pipe the mix on to the baking sheet and bake in the pre-heated oven for 20 minutes until golden brown. Leave to cool on a wire rack. The biscuits eat very well when sprinkled with caster sugar.

Variations

Lightly roll the shortbread mix about 1–2 cm (½–¾ in) thick and 20 cm (8 in) in diameter and place it in a flan ring. Mark it into eight pieces and prick all over with a fork before cooking. It will take about 30–35 minutes. Turn to pp. 174-75 for a photograph.

Chocolate Brownies

Here are two alternative chocolate brownie recipes (see pp.174–75). The first is very rich and tasty and can be used as petits fours or as a biscuit to go with ice-cream. Remember that when melting butter or chocolate, don't let it heat above room temperature.

SERVES 4

300 g (10 oz) caster sugar	225 g (8 oz) good quality plain chocolate
4 eggs	100 g (4 oz) hazel or pecan nuts,
225 g (8 oz) unsalted butter	chopped
75 g (3 oz) cocoa	100 g (4 oz) white chocolate, cut into
75 g (3 oz) plain flour	1 cm (½ in) chunks

Pre-heat the oven to 180–200°C/350–400°F/gas 4–6 and lightly grease a 20 cm (8 in) tin.

Beat together the sugar and eggs, making sure the sugar has completely dissolved. Melt the butter and whisk into the eggs. Sieve together the cocoa and flour and add to the butter and egg mix. Melt the chocolate in a bowl over a pan of warm water, then stir in. Add the chopped nuts and white chocolate. Turn the mix into the prepared tin and bake in the pre-heated oven for 30-40 minutes. Leave to cool, then cut into wedges or squares.

Quick Chocolate 'Brownies'

This recipe is even simpler and quicker to make than the one above, and it also goes well with ice-creams.

SERVES 4

200 g (7 oz) unsalted butter	175 g (6 oz) plain flour
50 g (2 oz) caster sugar	1 teaspoon of baking powder
1 teaspoon vanilla essence	50 g (2 oz) cornflakes, crushed
50 g (2 oz) chopped dates (Medjools are	25 g (1 oz) cocoa
best)	

Pre-heat the oven to 180–200°C/350–400°F/gas 4–6 and grease a 20 cm (8 in) tin.

Cream the butter and sugar together. Add all the other ingredients. Spoon the mixture into the prepared tin and bake in the pre-heated oven for 25–30 minutes.

Gingerbread Biscuits

These biscuits taste delicious if you add some chopped pecan nuts or dates – or both (see pp.174–75). If you are using dates or nuts, simply stir them in with the evaporated milk.

MAKES about 20

225 g (8 oz) plain flour
¼ teaspoon salt
2 teaspoons bicarbonate of soda
1 heaped teaspoon ground ginger
½ teaspoon cinnamon

50 g (2 oz) unsalted butter
100 g (4 oz) soft brown sugar
100 g (4 oz) golden syrup
1 tablespoon evaporated milk

Pre-heat the oven to180–200°C/350–400°F/gas 4–6 and grease two baking sheets.

Sift together the flour, salt, soda and spices. Heat the butter, sugar and syrup until dissolved. Leave to cool. Once cooled, mix into the dry ingredients with the evaporated milk to make a dough. Chill for 30 minutes.

Roll out the biscuit dough to about 5 mm (¼ in) thick and cut into fingers, circles or even gingerbread men! Place on the baking sheets, allowing a little space to spread. Bake in the pre-heated oven for 10–15 minutes.

Keeping an eye on the kitchen.

Cheesecake Cream

I like to serve this cheesecake recipe just as a cream. Of course, it can be spread on to a digestive biscuit base and covered with a fruit topping for a classic cheesecake. Using this recipe as a cream gives it many more options, from serving with summer fruits, poached fruits, chocolate cake (especially the one on p.170) or even ice-cream and raspberry sauce. It also eats very well if flavoured with honey and a drop of Irish whiskey. The other bonus is that it's quick and easy to make. The following quantities can be halved to make less.

SERVES 6–8

50 g (2 oz) caster sugar
450 g (1 lb) full fat soft cream cheese

600 ml (1 pint) double cream, lightly
    whipped

Beat the caster sugar into the cream cheese until the sugar has dissolved and creamed. Fold in the lightly whipped cream. It is important that the cream is only lightly whipped. This will prevent the cream from becoming over-beaten and separating when mixing with the cream cheese. Place the cheesecake in a suitable bowl or dish and set in the fridge for about an hour.

Once the cream has set, it can be served in the bowl or shaped between two spoons to serve on the plate.

Variations

Lots of other flavours can be added to this mix. One of my favourites is toffee. To make a toffee cream, simply add a tin of toffee (see p.164) to the cream cheese mix before folding in the whipped cream.

To make a chocolate version, melt 100–225 g (4–8 oz) of good quality plain chocolate, only allowing the chocolate to reach room temperature. The cream cheese must also be at room temperature and not chilled as this would set the cream when added. Simply mix the chocolate with the cream cheese and sugar, then fold in the whipped cream and set in the fridge. The 100 g (4 oz) is the minimum quantity of chocolate; your taste will determine the rest, but the more chocolate you add, the firmer the cream will be.

Poached Pears

This is an easy recipe to follow using simple quantities of two parts water to one part sugar, for example, 600 ml (1 pint) of water to 225 g (8 oz) of caster sugar. The best pears to use are Williams which have a good sweet taste and texture (see overleaf).

The pears can be used for many dishes like the Chocolate and Pear Brûlée (see p.152). They can also be made into a French classic, Poire Belle Hélène, which is poached pear with Vanilla Ice-cream (see p.190) and Chocolate Sauce (see p.216). This dish eats and looks very good if served in a Tuile Biscuit basket (see p.176). You could also use some poached pear in a knickerbockerglory glass layered with Vanilla Ice-cream (see p.190), pecan nuts, Chocolate Sauce (see p.216) and finished with Toffee Cream (see p.165). Now that is a rich pudding!

SERVES 6

6 pears   1.2 litres (2 pints) water
½ lemon   450 g (1 lb) caster sugar
1 vanilla pod or cinnamon stick
   (optional)

Peel the pears, then cut them in half. Remove the core either with a Parisienne scoop cutter or sharp knife. Also remove the vein of stalk running from the centre to the top of the pear by cutting diagonally either side of the vein. The pears can now be lightly rubbed with the lemon to prevent discoloration. Sit the pears in a pan with the lemon and vanilla or cinnamon if using, and cover with the water and caster sugar. Cover with greaseproof paper and bring to the boil. Simmer for a few minutes, then remove from the heat, leaving the pears to cool in the syrup.

The pears can now be kept chilled in the syrup with the lemon and vanilla or cinnamon in an airtight container until ready to be used.

ABOVE *Poached Pears (see p.181) and Poached Peaches (see p.184).*

OPPOSITE *Peach Melba (see p.185).*

Poached Peaches

Before poaching the peaches, they should be skinned. This is achieved by lightly scoring the peach skin all the way around the fruit with a sharp knife. Plunge the fruits into boiling water for a few seconds and then into cold water. This method is called blanching – very similar to skinning a tomato. The skin will now peel off.

These peaches eat very well as almost a pudding on their own or halved and used in a great Auguste Escoffier classic – Peach Melba (see preceding pages).

Serves 4

4–8 peaches, skinned	300 ml (10 fl oz) water
½ lemon	300 ml (10 fl oz) white wine
½ cinnamon stick (optional)	225 g (8 oz) caster sugar

Sit the skinned peaches into a pan with the lemon and cinnamon stick, if using. Pour the water and white wine on top and add the sugar. If you find this is not enough you can add either half or the same quantities again. Cover with some greaseproof paper and bring to the boil. Simmer the peaches for 4–5 minutes (3–4 minutes if they are very ripe and soft), then leave to cool in the syrup. The peaches are now ready and can be used straight away (even while still warm) or chilled. If you wish to keep them for some time then seal them in airtight jars.

When cooking the fruits if you have any problems keeping them submerged in the syrup, simply sit a plate on top to hold them in place.

Peach Melba

I like to serve Peach Melba in tuile baskets (see p.176). It's simply vanilla ice-cream (see p.190) topped with poached peaches and then finished with Melba Sauce. I also like to add whipped cream flavoured with fresh vanilla and sprinkled with toasted almonds, but this isn't essential. The Melba Sauce can be spooned on to the plate and the finished basket placed on top (see p.182).

Melba Sauce

Melba sauce, of course, is the sauce that goes with peach melba. There are many ways of making this raspberry sauce. This particular recipe gives a good balance of fruitiness to sweetness, but if you want a really quick version then simply boil 225 g (8 oz) of raspberry jam with 5 tablespoons of water and then strain through a sieve; or mix 225 g (8 oz) of fresh raspberries with 100 g (4 oz) of icing sugar, push through a sieve and add a squeeze of lemon juice. Well, there's two recipes. Now here's mine.

SERVES 4

225 g (8 oz) frozen raspberries, thawed   225 g (8 oz) raspberry jam
150 g (5 oz) caster sugar

Heat the raspberries with 50 g (2 oz) of the sugar until dissolved, then bring to the simmer. Push through a sieve to make a raspberry purée. Mix the purée with the remaining sugar and the jam and bring to the boil. Simmer for 3–4 minutes, then strain through a sieve. The sauce is ready and can be eaten hot or cold with many puddings.

Iced Cranachan Parfait

This is a Scottish recipe which is traditionally served at Halloween with soft red berries. It can also be made into an ice-cream by replacing the cream with Vanilla Ice-cream (see p.190), but this recipe is an iced terrine which eats well with a drizzle of honey, or Melba Sauce (see p.185) and fresh raspberries.

This recipe is for a 25 cm (10 in) terrine mould, but you can halve the quantities and use four individual ramekins.

SERVES 4

225 g (8 oz) caster sugar
8 egg yolks
600 ml (1 pint) double cream
4 teaspoons clear honey

175–225 g (6–8 oz) oatmeal, toasted
Whisky to taste (optional)
Clear honey to serve

Whisk the egg yolks and sugar until pale and the mixture trails off the whisk in thick ribbons. (This is easier if you place the bowl over a pan of warm water.) Pour on the cream and continue to whisk (cold) until the cream begins to thicken. Fold in the honey, toasted oatmeal and whisky to taste. Pour into the terrine or individual moulds and freeze until firm.

The cranachan can now be sliced and served.

Iced Chocolate Parfait

Sweet parfaits are like freezing a sweet sabayon. They take on a light ice-cream texture. The quantities here will fill a 25 cm (10 in) terrine mould, or you can use individual ramekins. The ingredients may look a little costly, but remember there are quite a lot of portions in a terrine – or you can simply make half the recipe. Serve the parfait as it is or with the rich Chocolate Sauce (see p.216), Orange Custard Sauce (see p.215) or Coffee Custard Sauce (see p.215). Of course, if you really want to finish this pudding with a little extra, then cover it with Chocolate Coating (see p.172). This gives the parfait a lovely finish and another texture.

SERVES 8

7 egg yolks
100 g (4 oz) caster sugar

175 g (6 oz) good quality plain chocolate
600 ml (1 pint) double cream

Line a 25 cm (10 in) terrine with cling film.

Whisk the egg yolks and sugar in a bowl over warm water until thick and at least doubled in volume. Melt the chocolate in a bowl over a pan of hot water, then mix with the yolks and sugar. Pour on the double cream and whisk until a soft peak is reached. The parfait is ready to freeze in the terrine or in individual moulds.

Note

The double cream can be whisked separately to soft peaks and then lightly folded with the chocolate mix.

Fresh Fruit Salad

Fresh fruit salad has endless combinations. It's basically prepared fruits all mixed together. The recipe here for fruit salad is just to give you an idea and a basic recipe to work from. Some fruits have a coarser texture and eat a lot better if just lightly softened in Stock Syrup (see p.217). Or you can try using Poached Peaches (see p.184) or Poached Pears (see p.181).

Any soft red fruits should always be added just before serving to prevent them colouring the other fruits.

One particular favourite of mine is summer fruit salad which is just poached blackberries, blueberries, redcurrants, blackcurrants, tayberries, strawberries and raspberries in a warm Stock Syrup (see p.217). The flavours and colours together are fantastic.

And here's just one more extra flavour. Use scissors to cut some thin strips of mint leaves and add them to the syrup. You get a lovely sweet mint flavour with every bite!

Of course, the best accompaniment to fresh fruit salad is simply pouring cream or even home-made Vanilla Ice-cream (see p.190).

SERVES 4

2 apples, peeled and cored	½ Ogen or Galia melon
50–75 g (2–3 oz) fresh pineapple chunks	1 large orange, segmented
300 ml (10 fl oz) Stock Syrup (either recipe) (see p.217)	2 kiwis, peeled and cut into 8 pieces each
2 plums, each cut into 8 segments	12 strawberries or raspberries
1 mango	1 banana, sliced

Cut the apples into 12 segments and mix them with the pineapple chunks. Bring the stock syrup to the boil and pour on to the apple and pineapple. While the syrup is still warm, add the plums. The mix should now be left to cool to room temperature.

Peel the mango, then cut it in half, removing the stone. Cut the mango into chunks. Repeat the same cutting process for the melon. Add the mango, melon, orange and kiwi to the other fruits in the syrup.

The fruit salad is now ready. The strawberries, raspberries and banana should not be added until the salad is about to be served.

Ice-creams

These recipes could just go on and on — there are so many different ice-creams and sorbets. They all eat well as puddings on their own or as accompaniments for other dishes.

Most of these recipes are derivatives of a basic vanilla ice-cream. In the vanilla recipe, a vanilla pod is used. This gives the ice-cream a real vanilla taste and when split and scraped leaves a black speckled finish to the cream. This can be substituted by using a few drops of strong vanilla essence or if you keep some caster sugar in an airtight container with a vanilla pod the vanilla aroma and flavour will stay with the sugar.

In most of the other ice-cream recipes, I suggest that you leave out the vanilla. The quantity of ingredients given in the basic vanilla recipe can, of course, be halved and all the other recipes can follow suit.

If you don't have an ice-cream machine, the mix can be left in a bowl and placed in the freezer, making sure it is stirred every 10–15 minutes until set.

If you're in a real hurry, there are a few short-cuts you can try for any of the recipes. You can buy a good quality vanilla ice-cream and add the other flavours so it's almost home-made or replace the vanilla ice-cream base with tinned custard using 600 ml (1 pint) for the equivalent recipe; tinned custards work really well as a base for ice-creams. If it tastes a little too rich and thick, add some milk or single cream to loosen the flavour and texture.

Vanilla Ice-cream

This is the base ice-cream which you can vary in an infinite number of ways!

SERVES 4–8

300 ml (10 fl oz) double cream
300 ml (10 fl oz) milk
1 vanilla pod or a few drops of vanilla
   essence

6 egg yolks
175 g (6 oz) caster sugar

Mix together the cream and milk in a pan. Split the vanilla pod lengthways and scrape the insides into the milk and cream, then add the scraped pod. Bring to the boil.

While they are heating, beat the egg yolks and sugar together until pale and light. This can be done in a food mixer. Pour on the milk and cream, stirring all the time until well blended. Stir from time to time until the ice-cream mix has cooled. Remove the vanilla pod.

Once cooled, the mix is ready to be churned in the ice-cream maker. If you have made the full recipe, you'll need to churn it in two batches. Pour the mix into the machine and begin to turn. The ice-cream will take about 20–30 minutes and will have thickened and increased in volume. Don't leave the mix turning until completely frozen and set as this will be over-churned and slightly grainy in texture. Take out when thick and starting to freeze and then finish in the freezer. This will give you a lovely silky smooth texture.

If you don't have an ice-cream machine, simply turn the mixture into a freezer tray or bowl and freeze, turning regularly until set.

Clockwise, starting from the top right:
Vanilla Ice-cream; Toffee Ice-cream (see p.200);
Maple Syrup and Pecan Nut Ice-cream (see p.197);
Coconut Ice-cream (see p.195);
Raspberry Soft Fruit Ice-cream (see p.204);
Chocolate Ice-cream (see p.193).

Banana Ice-cream

Try this ice-cream with Chocolate Sauce (see p.216) and warm pancakes.

SERVES 4–8

1 quantity Vanilla Ice-cream (see p.190)
225 g (8 oz) peeled ripe bananas
A few drops of lemon juice

1–2 tablespoons banana liqueur
(optional)

First you need to make the vanilla ice-cream base. Once made and still warm, peel and chop the bananas and toss them in the lemon juice to help them keep their colour. Then add them to the base. This can now be blitzed in a food processor and then pushed through a sieve. Stir in the liqueur, if using. The ice-cream can now be finished in an ice-cream machine, then frozen.

Chocolate Ice-cream

This is a delicious ice-cream with lots of very adult alternatives (see p.191)!

SERVES 4–8

1 quantity Vanilla Ice-cream (see p.190), made with 100 g (4 oz) caster sugar and without the vanilla pod

175 g (6 oz) good quality plain chocolate, grated

Follow the vanilla base recipe using only 100 g (4 oz) of caster sugar. Once the milk and cream have been brought to the boil, pour on to the grated chocolate and stir. This will melt the chocolate. Taste before churning to check the chocolate flavour is strong enough. Continue with the basic recipe.

Variations

This ice-cream has many alternatives.

1 Add some rum to taste.

2 Add some Cointreau or Grand Marnier to taste.

3 Add 2–3 tablespoons of marmalade for chocolate and orange ice-cream (and maybe a little Cointreau too!).

4 Add some broken Honeycomb (see p.208) just at the end of churning.

Christmas Pudding Ice-cream

This is a great Christmas pudding alternative to surprise your guests. It eats really well on its own or as an accompaniment to a tart or flan. The other great way to use this recipe is to make it from your left-over pudding, turning it into a new dish.

For this recipe I'm using a home-made custard as the base, but here is a quick and simple alternative: if you buy a 450 g (1 lb) Christmas pudding and just chop it all up, then stir it into two tins of ready-made custard you have an instant mix for Christmas Pudding Ice-cream. It can be as simple as that!

SERVES 4–8

450 g (1 lb) Christmas pudding   1.2 litres (2 pints) Custard Sauce
                                               (see p.215)

The Christmas pudding can be used straight from the packet. All you need to do is simply cut the pudding into slices and then into small rough dice. If you are using the left-overs from Christmas lunch, then just break it down into crumble pieces. Now all you have to do is stir in the custard and mix for a minute or two. Pour some of the mix into an ice-cream machine (making sure the Christmas pudding pieces are equally distributed) and allow to turn. Once the cream has started to thicken and cream, turn the ice-cream out and finish setting in the freezer. If you overturn the ice-cream it will break down the pudding and become darker and slightly bitter in taste. Repeat the same process for the remaining mix.

To re-create the pudding theme and shape, just set the ice-cream in a pudding basin and freeze. Once turned out, you have a Christmas pudding with a difference! I also like to pour maple syrup over the top to enrich it even more.

If you don't have an ice-cream maker, pour the mix on to a tray and set in the freezer, turning from time to time until frozen. The ice-cream doesn't quite have the full volume or texture but still tastes good.

Coconut Ice-cream

This ice-cream can take on loads of combinations (see p.191). It can be coated in chocolate, almost like making your own 'taste of paradise', mixed with chopped pineapple, made into a Piña Colada pudding, or even served with Pineapple Fritters (see p.148) and Chocolate Sauce (see p.216). If you don't have a fresh coconut, just replace it with 50 g (2 oz) of desiccated coconut.

Serves 4–8

¼ fresh coconut
175 ml (6 fl oz) double cream
250 ml (8 fl oz) milk

100 g (4 oz) caster sugar
5 egg yolks
200 ml (7 fl oz) coconut milk

Crack the coconut and peel off a quarter of the white coconut flesh. Chop the flesh finely and mix with the cream and milk. Bring to the boil. While the milk mix is coming to the boil, whisk the sugar and egg yolks together in a large bowl until pale and light. Pour over the boiling milk, then place the bowl over a pan of hot water and stir until thickened. Blitz in a blender until the coconut is shredded, then leave to cool. Add the coconut milk and churn in the ice-cream machine until beginning to freeze, then turn into a freezer container and freeze until firm.

If you don't have an ice-cream maker, pour the mix on to a tray and set in the freezer, turning from time to time until frozen.

Crème Fraîche Ice-cream

Using crème fraîche in any ice-cream really lifts the taste of other flavours. But using it as a main flavouring gives a basic vanilla ice-cream a really good bite. For every 300 ml (10 fl oz) of Vanilla Ice-cream (see p.190) you will need to add at least 150 ml (5 fl oz) of crème fraîche while the mixture is still liquid. This will give quite a strong taste. After that it's really up to you. If you want it stronger, simply start to add a spoonful at a time until you have the flavour you want. To make the flavour a little sharper, then also add 1 tablespoon of natural yoghurt to the mix.

The other alternative is to mix a tin of custard with 150 ml (5 fl oz) of crème fraîche and you have instant ice-cream mix.

Honey and Whisky Ice-cream

It is up to you how much whisky you like to add to this dessert – I use about two measures.

SERVES 4–8

1 quantity Vanilla Ice-cream (see p.190), made without caster sugar (vanilla pod optional)

350 g (12 oz) jar clear honey
Whisky to taste

This is really easy to make. Simply mix the honey with the egg yolks from the vanilla recipe and beat them together. Follow the method, adding the whisky to taste before turning.

Lemon Curd Ice-cream

This ice-cream is lovely and rich and eats beautifully as a pudding on its own or as an extra for a Steamed Lemon Sponge (see p.156). The ice-cream is superb if totally home-made, but also works very well if you substitute the fresh lemon curd for a jar of lemon curd.

SERVES 4–6

1 quantity Lemon Curd (see p.208) or 1 × 350 g (12 oz) jar of lemon curd	2 large tablespoons crème fraîche 1 large tablespoon natural yoghurt

Mix the cooled lemon curd with the crème fraîche and yoghurt and churn into ice-cream. It's as simple as that!

Maple Syrup and Pecan Nut Ice-cream

You need to make the base with less sugar so that the maple syrup does not make the ice-cream too rich (see p.191).

SERVES 6–8

1 quantity Vanilla Ice-cream (see p.190), using only 75 g (3 oz) of caster sugar (vanilla pod optional)	300 g (11 oz) maple syrup 50–75 g (2–3 oz) pecan nuts, chopped

Follow the recipe and method of the vanilla ice-cream using half the sugar quantity. This will allow the sweetness of the maple syrup to work without becoming over-rich. Once the vanilla base is made and cooled, add the maple syrup and begin to churn the ice-cream. The pecan nuts should only be added to the mix during the last few minutes of churning. If they are added too early, the nuts will break down and also discolour the cream.

Marmalade Ice-cream

This ice-cream is rich, tasty and wonderful! It goes really well with Steamed Orange Sponge (see p.158) or Steamed Chocolate Sponge (see p.160). It's best to buy a good quality coarse marmalade to give a strong orange taste.

SERVES 6–8

1 quantity Vanilla Ice-cream (see p.190), made without the vanilla pod

1 × 350 g (12 oz) jar coarse marmalade

Follow the recipe for vanilla ice-cream. Stir the boiled cream and milk into the egg yolks and sugar, then add the marmalade and then continue to follow the method.

There's always time for a cup of tea.

Rice Pudding Ice-cream with Raspberry Jam Sauce

I love baked rice pudding. It was one of my favourites at home with the lovely skin on top. Creamed rice pudding is also one of my favourites, especially with raspberry jam spooned on top. Well, I thought I would come up with the opposite. Rice pudding ice-cream with warm jam sauce. It works really well and when you tell your guests they've got rice pudding and jam sauce, this will definitely surprise them. This ice-cream also works very well in a Rice Pudding Arctic Roll with Raspberry Coulis (see p.205). Remember, you can always substitute the fresh vanilla base for a tin of custard to make the recipe quicker.

SERVES 4–8

For the Rice Pudding

600 ml (1 pint) milk
15 g (½ oz) unsalted butter

40 g (1½ oz) caster sugar
50 g (2 oz) short-grain pudding rice

For the Ice-cream

600 ml (1 pint) Vanilla Ice-cream (see p.190), made with a pinch of freshly

grated nutmeg and without the vanilla pod or vanilla essence

For the Raspberry Jam Sauce

175 g (6 oz) raspberry jam

2–3 tablespoons water

Bring the milk, butter and sugar to the boil. Add the rice and bring to the simmer. Simmer and cook gently, stirring frequently, until the rice is over-cooked; this will take about 25–30 minutes. The rice has to be close to breaking/purée point to prevent it from becoming crunchy when made into ice-cream.

Once the rice pudding has cooled, mix with the vanilla base and churn in the ice-cream machine for 15–20 minutes until thickened and increased in volume. The rice pudding ice-cream can now be set in the freezer.

To make the sauce, just warm the jam and water together until they reach a thick sauce consistency. If the jam is still too thick, then add a little more water to correct the consistency. The sauce can also be pushed through a sieve to leave a smooth, clear jam sauce, ready to be poured over the creamy rich ice-cream.

Strawberry or Raspberry Ripple Ice-creams

These are lovely, home-made ripple ices that make a delicious pudding served in a Tuile Biscuit basket (see p.176) with fresh cream or Custard Sauce (see p.215). The ice-cream has a wonderful flavour with the tartness of the raspberry or strawberry to excite your tastebuds. The quantities to follow are two-thirds ice-cream to one-third fruit, so whatever amount you want, if you follow these guidelines it will always work. This ice-cream also works very well in an Arctic Roll (see p.205).

SERVES 4–8

450 ml (15 fl oz) Vanilla Ice-cream (see p.190)

150 ml (5 fl oz) Raspberry or Strawberry Coulis (see p.207)

Make the ice-cream, churn the mixture and place in a freezer container. Spoon the coulis on top and then lightly fold the coulis into the ice-cream. This will give you red streaks through the ice-cream. Set in the freezer.

Toffee Ice-cream

Here's another use for my simple toffee mix (see p.191).

SERVES 4–8

600 ml (1 pint) Vanilla Ice-cream (see p.190)

1 × 400 g (14 oz) tin of toffee (see p.164)

Follow the recipe for vanilla ice-cream, stirring in the toffee once you have made the custard. Turn the mix in an ice-cream machine.

Chocolate and Toffee Bockerglory

This has to be the ultimate in sticky puddings. The combinations are unlimited and that's the beauty of cooking, there's no limits! So rather than give you a strict recipe, I'll just give you some ideas of how it can be put together. It's best to make it in tall glasses or deep bowls.

Remember, to make this dish you don't have to go through the process of making every component. Most, if not all, of these can be found in most food stores, and you can vary the ingredients however you like. So if you want to have a try with no effort involved, use some Jamaican ginger cake diced up and mixed with chocolate or coffee sauce, top with some chocolate and vanilla ice-cream, more sauce and finish with almonds and chocolate.

To make chocolate shavings, take a bar of good, rich dark chocolate and turn it on its side, looking at the width of the bar. From top to bottom scrape along the chocolate with the edge of a palette knife. This will create shavings to sprinkle on top of your desserts.

SERVES as many as you need

Chocolate Fudge Cake (see p.168), chocolate sponge or Jamaican ginger cake
Pecan Nut Sauce (see p.168)
Chocolate Ice-cream (see p.193)
Toffee Ice-cream (see p.200)
Chocolate Sauce (see p.216)

Double cream, whipped
Flaked almonds, toasted
Chocolate shavings
Sprigs of fresh mint to decorate
Icing sugar for sprinkling
Wafer biscuits to serve

Dice the cake into 1 cm (½ in) pieces and mix them with some of the pecan nut sauce. Spoon the cake into the glasses. Next spoon some chocolate ice-cream on top and follow that with some toffee or vanilla ice-cream. Pour cold chocolate sauce on top. Cover with whipped cream and sprinkle over the toasted almonds and chocolate shavings. This pudding can now be served with a sprig of mint on top, a dusting of icing sugar, a long spoon and a biscuit. How does that sound?

Black Forest Arctic Roll

Black Forest gâteau is still a popular dessert. The flavours of chocolate, cherries and cream marry well – if the dessert is well made! With this dish I've taken all those flavours and turned them into a tasty and fun pudding. The sponge can also be used for a chocolate Swiss roll. You'll need a cylinder in which to freeze the ice-cream into shape. I use a piece of plastic piping from a hardware store, about 15 cm (6 in) long by 6 cm (2½ in) diameter. Wrap cling film securely round one end. The whole dish might sound a bit involved, but you can save time by using a ready-made ice-cream and tinned cherries if you like, so have a go!

SERVES 4–6

For the Chocolate Sponge

3 eggs

75 g (3 oz) caster sugar

50 g (2 oz) plain flour

15 g (½ oz) cornflour

25 g (1 oz) cocoa

For the Arctic Roll

175–225 g (6–8 oz) fresh cherries or
    tinned cherries

50 ml (2 fl oz) Stock Syrup (see p.217)

Kirsch (optional)

600 ml (1 pint) Vanilla Ice-cream,
    prepared and churned (see p.190)

3–4 tablespoons black cherry jam

Pre-heat the oven to 180°C/350°F/gas 4 and grease and line a Swiss roll tin.

Whisk the eggs and sugar together until pale and fluffy. Sift together the dry ingredients, then fold into the egg mix a little at a time. Spread the mix evenly in the prepared tin and bake in the pre-heated oven for 10–15 minutes. No colour is needed on this sponge, just set the mix. Allow to cool.

Stone the cherries and sit them in a pan with the syrup and a splash of kirsch, if using. Bring the cherries to the simmer and cook for 1–2 minutes. Leave to cool. Once cooled, mix half the cherries with the vanilla ice-cream. Stand the cylinder up, making sure the base has been well cling filmed. Spoon the ice-cream into the cylinder and set in the freezer.

Sieve the liquid from the remaining cherries and bring the syrup to the boil with the cherry jam. The liquid will now be a lot thicker. Mix the cherries with the syrup.

Turn the chocolate sponge off the tray but leave it still attached to the paper. Brush the sponge with some cherry jam. Remove the cling film from one end of the ice-cream and pour hot water on to the cylinder to loosen and remove the ice-cream. Sit the ice-cream on the sponge and roll until the sponge meets, creating a cylinder and cutting off any excess. Roll the whole thing in cling film and freeze for 30 minutes.

To serve, remove from the freezer and take off the cling film before cutting into portions. Each plate can be garnished with a spoon of cherries in syrup.

Variations

To add an extra garnish for a special occasion, simply shape some whipped cream and scrape a palette knife across some dark or milk chocolate to garnish with rolled pieces. Finish with sprigs of mint and lightly dust with icing sugar.

Black Forest Arctic Roll.

Knickerbockerglory

This Knickerbockerglory can be made by the same method as the Chocolate and Toffee Bockerglory. Instead of using the chocolate sponge, sandwich the Swiss roll sponge (see p.205) with raspberry jam and then cut into dice and place in the bottom of the glass. Spoon in some summer fruits mixed with a Fruit Coulis (see p.207). Next is the ice-cream. I like to use two ice-creams, starting with some Vanilla (see p.190), then adding more fruits before spooning in some Raspberry or Strawberry Ice-cream (see p.200). Finish the bockerglory with some more fruits and then whipped cream, chocolate and mint (see p.147).

    It's awesome, good luck!

Soft Fruit Ice-cream

These are quick and easy to make. All you need is a sweet Fruit Purée (see p.207) and some crème fraîche. Crème fraîche is fresh cream that has been treated with a special culture which almost sours the cream and gives it a longer life. It works really well in ice-creams, giving a full flavour. Soft summer fruits, such as strawberries or raspberries (see p.191), work beautifully in this recipe, but there is no need to wait until the soft fruit season to make them. The easy alternative is simply to take a tin of almost any fruit – peaches, pears, blackberries or whatever – and purée them in their own syrup. Add some icing sugar to increase the sweetness, then add 2–3 heaped tablespoons of crème fraîche. Now you have a quick and easy ice-cream, just churn it in the machine and it's ready.

SERVES 4

1 quantity Fruit Purée (see p.207)   2–3 heaped tablespoons crème fraîche
150 ml (5 fl oz) Stock Syrup (see p.217)

Mix all ingredients together and churn in an ice-cream machine for 15–20 minutes until thick. If you don't have a machine, then spoon into a bowl and freeze, stirring every 5–10 minutes until set.

Rice Pudding Arctic Roll

This recipe is a copy of the Black Forest Arctic Roll. Simply make the rice pudding ice-cream and freeze in the plastic cylinder. Then you can create the Arctic roll with the Swiss roll sponge. Strawberry Ripple Ice-cream (see p.200) also works. I'm going to serve it with some Raspberry Coulis (see p.207).

SERVES 4–8

For the Sponge

3 eggs, separated
100 g (4 oz) caster sugar

75 g (3 oz) plain flour
25 g (1 oz) cornflour

For the Arctic Roll

Raspberry jam
Rice Pudding Ice-cream (see p.199)
Raspberry Coulis (see p.207)
Fresh raspberries (optional)

Double cream
1 sprig of fresh mint
Icing sugar, sifted

Pre-heat the oven to 180°/350°F/gas 4 and butter and line a Swiss roll tin.

Whisk the egg yolks and 75 g (3 oz) of sugar together until thick and creamy. Whisk the egg whites with the remaining sugar to a firm meringue. Sift the plain flour and cornflour together, then lightly fold into the egg yolk mix. Carefully fold in the egg white. Spread the mix into the prepared tray and cook in the pre-heated oven for 15–20 minutes. Remove from the oven and allow to cool.

Spread some raspberry jam on to the sponge, keeping the golden brown top for the outside. Remove the ice-cream from the cylinder by running the plastic under hot water for a few seconds. Sit the ice-cream on top of the sponge and roll around, cutting off any excess sponge. Roll in cling film and freeze for at least 30 minutes.

Once frozen, remove the cling film and cut into four portions. Garnish each portion with Raspberry Coulis and fresh raspberries (optional). It's also nice served with thick fresh cream, a sprig of mint and lightly dusted with icing sugar.

Fruit Sorbets

Sorbets are a light and refreshing alternative to ice-cream. They are good to have as a middle course palate cleanser or as a dessert.

You can use any soft fruits you like – strawberries, raspberries, pineapple, mango, melon – and whichever stock syrup you prefer.

SERVES 4–8

225 g (8 oz) fruit   Juice of ½ lemon
150 ml (5 fl oz) Stock Syrup (see p.217)

Simply mix the fruits with the syrup and blitz in a blender, then push through a sieve. You now have a fruit syrup. Add the lemon juice to this to help lift the flavours. Churn in an ice-cream machine for 20 minutes and freeze, or turn into a freezer tray and place in the freezer, stirring and turning every 20–30 minutes until frozen.

Variations

If you want to make an apple or pear sorbet, simply peel, core and chop the fruits, mix with the lemon juice and cook in the stock syrup until softened. Then blitz and push through a sieve and leave to cool before making into sorbet.

Chocolate Sorbet

You're going to love this recipe. It's easy to make, rich in taste and also very refreshing.

SERVES 4

25 g (1 oz) cocoa
450 ml (15 fl oz) water

150 g (5 oz) good quality plain chocolate
150 g (5 oz) caster sugar

Simmer the cocoa in the water for 5 minutes. While simmering, chop the chocolate. Pour the water and cocoa on to the chocolate and sugar and stir in. Once cool, churn in the ice-cream machine until thickened, then freeze.

Fruit Purées or Coulis

Fruit purées, or coulis, are used for many things, particularly bases for sorbets, as sweet sauces and as flavourings in mousses. The French term coulis literally means sieved and this method is used for soft fruits such as strawberries, raspberries and blackcurrants. Because of the sharpness in the flavour, the fruits may need to be mixed with icing sugar. These quantities are good guidelines; you can vary them to suit the tartness of the fruit. They go very well with ice-creams and iced parfaits.

MAKES about 225 g (8 oz)

225 g (8 oz) soft fruit
50 g (2 oz) icing sugar, sifted

A few drops of lemon juice

Blitz the fruit and sugar together in a food processer, then push through a sieve. If the flavour is still too tart, simply add more icing sugar to taste. The consistency will be of a thick sauce which can be thinned down if needed with some Stock Syrup (see p.217), or some more icing sugar blended with a little water. A few drops of lemon will help lift the flavour of the fruit.

Honeycomb

Honeycomb is, of course, the filling in a Crunchie bar. This recipe could be used to make your own, but I like to break the honeycomb into pieces and add it to a chocolate ice-cream just at the end of churning. This gives you a lovely crunchy texture in the ice-cream. It's also nice just broken and sprinkled on top of an ice-cream pudding.

To make honeycomb you need to boil the sugar, so do take care as it reaches very high temperatures. You must always make sure that you have a very clean, large pan for this recipe and also a sugar thermometer will be needed.

SERVES 4–6

2 tablespoons water	50 g (2 oz) golden syrup
225 g (8 oz) demerara sugar	15 g (½ oz) unsalted butter
225 g (8 oz) granulated sugar	1 tablespoon bicarbonate of soda

Pour the water into a saucepan, add the sugars, golden syrup and butter. Bring the mix to the boil and continue to cook to a small crack temperature. This is 138–140°C/280–284°F. The sugar mix will have a rich golden colour. Add the bicarbonate of soda; this will lift the sugar and create a light airy texture. Pour the honeycomb mix into a greased 23 × 28 cm (9 × 11 in) tray and allow to set. Once cooled and set the honeycomb is ready and can be kept in an airtight container.

Lemon Curd

Lemon curd eats very well just on toast or teacakes. I like to use it for Lemon Curd Ice-cream (see p.197) or as a sauce for steamed sponges.

This recipe is very rich with a high butter content. If you prefer, you can cut the butter down to 100 g (4 oz) and also cut down by 1 egg yolk. The lemon curd will still work without being over-rich and will have a slightly more fluid consistency. There are two alternative methods.

225 g (8 oz) caster sugar
225 g (8 oz) unsalted butter

Finely grated zest and juice of 3 lemons
5 egg yolks

For method 1, sit the sugar, butter, lemon juice and zest in a bowl and stir over a pan of simmering water. Once the butter has melted, beat vigorously until well combined. Beat in the egg yolks and continue to cook and stir for 15–20 minutes until the curd has thickened. Pour into a clean jar and cover with waxed paper or cling film. Once cooled, seal tightly and keep in the fridge. This should keep for at least two weeks.

For method 2, whisk the sugar and egg yolks together until light and creamy. Melt the butter with the lemon zest and juice and add to the mix. Cook, stirring, in a bowl over a pan of simmering water until thickened; this will also take about 15–20 minutes.

Lemon Jelly

This is a simple home-made jelly. The lemon jelly goes very well with ice-cream. I like to serve either the Vanilla (see p.190), Lemon Curd (see p.197) or Crème Fraîche Ice-cream (see p.196) with it. This is really a good, fun dessert to offer your guests at a dinner party – jelly and ice-cream!

The recipe also works well if the lemons are replaced or mixed with limes for a different flavour.

600 ml (1 pint) water
275 g (10 oz) caster sugar

Finely grated zest and juice of 5 lemons
7–8 leaves of gelatine

Warm and dissolve the sugar in the water on the stove with the lemon juice and zest. Keep on the heat for 2–3 minutes. Remove from the stove. Soak the gelatine leaves in cold water until they become soft and jelly-like. Remove the gelatine and squeeze out any excess water. Stir the gelatine into the warm, sweet lemon water until dissolved. The sweet jelly water can now be left to cool, stirring occasionally. Once cooled, the jelly can be poured into a presentation bowl and left to set in the fridge.

Home-made Blackberry Jam

In this recipe there are two alternatives for the quantity of sugar, but both work by the same method. The difference is quite simple. If equal amounts of sugar and fruit are used, more syrup is made from the sugar. Also, by using a preserving sugar containing pectin, the jam is guaranteed to set. By using half the sugar content, less syrup is made and so consequently a thicker more 'jammy' texture and not quite as sweet taste is the result. I prefer to make the jam with half of the sugar content to achieve a stronger natural taste of the fruits, although jam made in this way will only last for a maximum of two weeks.

This is a basic recipe which can be applied to most soft fruits such as raspberries, strawberries and cherries. However, sharp, firmer fruits, such as blackcurrants, will require more sugar to balance the acidity.

These berries obviously have seeds so if you prefer to make jam without them, simply strain through a sieve once.

If you intend to eat the jam within a week or two, simply allow the jam to cool, place in warmed jam jars, leave to cool, then chill. The sugar and pectin are both natural preservatives so the jam will keep perfectly fresh.

If you want to store the jams for longer, you'll need to sterilize them. Sterilize the jars first by covering them with cold water in a large pan, then bringing the water to the boil. Leave to boil for 10–15 minutes, then remove and dry. The glass should be warm before adding the hot jam to prevent the jar from shattering. Once the jars are filled, covered and sealed, you can sterilize them further by sitting the jars on a wire rack or cloth in a large pan and almost covering with water. Bring the water to the boil, then repeat the process. Store the jam in a cool, dark place, or chill it; it will last almost indefinitely.

MAKES about 900 g (2 lb)

900 g (2 lb) blackberries   Juice of 1 lemon
450 g (1 lb) or 900 g (2 lb) sugar with
    pectin

Carefully rinse the blackberries, making sure you do not damage the fruits. Warm the sugar in a large, heavy-based pan over a low heat; this will take 1–2 minutes. Add the fruits and the sugar will begin to dissolve. Once some liquid is forming, turn up the heat and bring to the boil, stirring gently. Stir in the lemon juice. As the mix is heating, some froth and impurities will begin to rise to the top. This froth should be skimmed off. Once boiling rapidly, continue to cook for about 6–7 minutes. The jam should have reached the temperature of 105°C/220°F. With the pectin in the sugar this will be at setting point. If you don't have a sugar thermometer, simply sit a spoonful of mix on a saucer and set in the fridge. Once cold and touched, the jam should have a jellied, wrinkled texture and is now ready to pour into the jars and cover with waxed paper. Allow to cool before closing the lids. The jam should be kept in a dark, cool place or chilled for extra life.

Shortcrust and Sweet Crust Pastry

This recipe really is short! In ingredients and in texture.

This quantity is really the minimum amount to make for a good texture. The beauty of this pastry is that it freezes so well to be used later.

MAKES about 400 g (14 oz)

175 g (6 oz) unsalted butter, chopped	4 tablespoons cold water
240 g (8½ oz) plain flour	

Rub the butter into the flour until a crumble effect is achieved. Add the water and fold in very lightly until the pastry is only just beginning to form and bind. Press the pastry between two sheets of cling film. The pastry will have a marbled look; this indicates just how short the pastry is going to be.

Variations

This pastry works very well with the Fillet of Mackerel with Caramelized Onions and Sweet Peppers (see p.26) or as a savoury or sweet flan base. To make sweet pastry, simply add 50 g (2 oz) of sifted icing sugar to the flour.

Puff Pastry

This recipe is useful for all kinds of desserts and for savoury pies as well. It's very satisfying to make your own pastry, but you can resort to the chill cabinet of your supermarket if you are short of time.

MAKES about 450 g (1 lb)

225 g (8 oz) unsalted butter
225 g (8 oz) strong plain flour
A pinch of salt

150 ml (5 fl oz) cold water
A few drops of lemon juice

Cut off 50 g (2 oz) of the butter, melt it then leave it to cool. The remaining block should be left out to soften. Sift the flour and salt together into a large bowl and make a well in the centre. Pour the water, lemon juice and cooled, melted butter into the well in the flour and gently fold in the flour to make a pliable dough. Wrap in cling film and allow to rest in the fridge for 20 minutes.

On a lightly floured board, roll out the pastry from four sides, leaving a lump in the centre. The dough should look like a crossroads. The remaining block of butter should have softened to a similar texture to the dough; it should be easy to roll without melting but not so hard that it will break the pastry.

Sit the butter on the centre lump of the dough (A) and fold over each pastry flap (B). Pat the pastry into a 30 × 15 cm (12 × 6 in) rectangle and leave to rest in the fridge for 10–15 minutes.

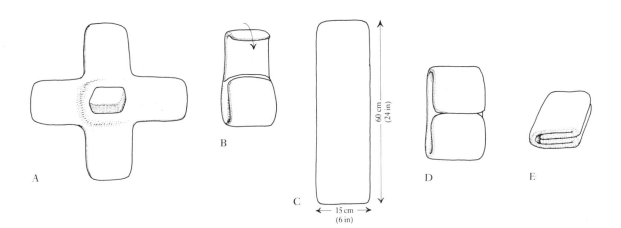

A   B   C   15 cm (6 in)   60 cm (24 in)   D   E

Roll out the pastry lengthways to make it double in length to about 60 cm (24 in) but the same width (C). Fold in both ends to the centre (D) and then fold once more (E). This is called a double turn and should be completed a further three times, each time rolling out the same length and then finishing with a double turn. Always roll with the folded edge on the left, and always leave to rest for 20–30 minutes in the fridge before each turn. The pastry should now be rested for at least 30 minutes in the fridge before using.

This puff pastry is perfect for the savoury tarts (see p.120). To make the pastry cases, butter and flour your chosen moulds: 25 cm (10 in) ring or six 10 cm (4 in) rings. Roll the pastry out thinly and line the moulds, leaving any excess turned over the sides of the rings. Sit the cases on a baking sheet and rest in the fridge for 10–15 minutes. Line with greaseproof paper and baking beans or rice. Bake in a pre-heated oven at 200°C/400°F/gas 6 for 15–20 minutes until the pastry is baked and golden. Remove the paper and beans, then use a sharp knife to trim off any excess pastry around the tart cases, leaving the cases in the pastry rings.

Almond Paste or Frangipane

This almond paste is the recipe which is used to make Bakewell Tart, that old favourite nursery pudding. The mixture freezes well, or you can make it in smaller amounts, just maintaining the same proportions.

SERVES 4–8

225 g (8 oz) unsalted butter, cold
225 g (8 oz) caster sugar
175 g (6 oz) ground almonds

50 g (2 oz) plain flour
4 eggs

Cream together the butter and sugar until almost white. Mix together the ground almonds and flour. Add one egg at a time to the butter and sugar mixture, sprinkling a handful of ground almonds and flour at the same time. This helps the butter and sugar cream to accept the eggs. Once all the eggs have been added, just continue to fold in the remaining almond and flour mixture.

Cook as directed in the recipes.

Banana and Toffee Cream Pancakes

Here's a great alternative for Shrove Tuesday! Of course, the pancakes can also be used in many other puddings, especially when served with ice-creams. How does warm pancakes with vanilla ice-cream and hot jam sauce sound?

SERVES 4–6

4 bananas   Icing sugar, sifted
1 quantity Toffee Cream (see p.165)   A few sprigs of fresh mint
Maple syrup (optional)

For the Pancakes

100 g (4 oz) plain flour   300 ml (10 fl oz) milk
A pinch of salt   25 g (1 oz) unsalted butter, melted
1 egg   Vegetable oil

Sift the flour and salt together. Beat the egg into the milk and whisk into the flour. Add the melted butter. The pancake mix is now ready. Pre-heat a 25 cm (10 in) pancake pan and trickle some vegetable oil into the pan, making sure the oil has very lightly covered the pan. Add a thin layer of pancake mix to the pan. Cook for 15–20 seconds until golden, then flip over and cook for a further 10–15 seconds on the other side. The pancake is now ready. Repeat the same process until all the mix is finished.

Peel the bananas and cut diagonally into thick slices. Sit the pancake on the plate and fold in half, keeping the semi-circular side facing you. Overlap the banana slices on one quarter of the pancake and spoon some toffee cream on top. Fold the other half of pancake over the cream, leaving a triangular-shaped pudding on the plate. Sprinkle with maple syrup, if using, and dust icing sugar around the plate. Garnish with a sprig of mint.

Variations

Try dusting the sliced bananas with icing sugar and glazing them under the grill until the sugar has caramelized, then use them in the pancakes.

Anglaise (Fresh Custard) Sauces

This recipe is for a fresh custard or anglaise sauce, which can act as a base for so many different flavours. You must only ever serve it warm, not boiled, as this will scramble the egg yolks in the cream mix. The fresh vanilla is optional and can be omitted when using other flavours. To have the flavour of vanilla always at hand, keep a vanilla pod in your jar of caster sugar; the aroma from the pod will impregnate the sugar.

MAKES 750 ml (1¼ pints)

8 egg yolks
75 g (3 oz) caster sugar
1 vanilla pod, split (optional)

300 ml (10 fl oz) milk
300 ml (10 fl oz) double cream

Beat the egg yolks and sugar together in a bowl until well blended. Split and scrape the insides of the vanilla pod, if using, into the milk and cream and bring to the boil. Sit the bowl over a pan of hot water and whisk the cream into the egg mix. As the egg yolks warm, the cream will thicken to create a custard. Keep stirring until it coats the back of a spoon. Remove the bowl from the heat. The custard can now be served warm or stirred occasionally until it cools. Serve warm or cold.

Variations

For Lemon Custard Sauce, add the pared rind of 2 lemons, not the pith, to the milk and cream when heating, then leave it in the mix throughout the cooking process. Once the custard has thickened, add the juice of one lemon and taste. If the lemon flavour is not strong enough, simply add more lemon juice to taste. Strain the custard through a sieve.

For Orange Custard Sauce, add the pared rind of 2 oranges to the milk and cream when heating, then cook as for the basic recipe. Orange juice will not be used in this recipe. To lift the flavour of the sauce, try adding a few drops of Cointreau or Grand Marnier.

For Rum Custard Sauce, add some rum to taste at the end of cooking the vanilla custard. This goes very well with Pineapple Fritters (see p.148). Desiccated coconut could also be added to this recipe during the cooking process and/or coconut milk added at the end.

Coffee Custard Sauce can be made by replacing the vanilla pod with 2 teaspoons of good fresh ground coffee and cook as for the vanilla base recipe. Once the coffee custard has completely cooled just strain through a sieve to remove any excess granules.

Chocolate Sauce

This chocolate sauce is lovely and rich in flavour and texture. It eats really well either hot or cold and goes with so many different puddings. Chocolate must be very carefully treated. If overheated, the chocolate will become split and grainy. Not every commercial chocolate works in cooking, but I have always found Bournville to be quite a safe bet.

SERVES 4–8

200 g (7 oz) good quality plain chocolate, finely chopped

25 g (1 oz) unsalted butter, chilled and diced

150 ml (5 fl oz) milk

2 tablespoons double cream

25 g (1 oz) caster sugar

Mix together the chocolate and butter. Boil the milk, cream and sugar and pour on to the chocolate mix. Stir the mixture until completely melted, but do not allow it to re-boil. The chocolate sauce is now ready. Serve warm or cold – the cooler the temperature, the thicker the sauce.

Stock Syrups

These syrups have many uses. They are a great base for sorbets, for poaching, and for steeping fruits. Any spirits or liqueurs can be added; even teabags or fresh tea can be added for sorbets or ice-creams. I'm going to give two recipes. The first is very basic and the second is almost a dish on its own and packed with flavour. Both keep almost indefinitely if chilled. The fruit stock syrup is good to use in a fresh fruit salad and can also have mint added to take on another flavour.

For Simple Stock Syrup

600 ml (1 pint) water   350 g (12 oz) caster sugar

For Fruit Stock Syrup

600 ml (1 pint) water   Pared zest and juice of 2 oranges
350 g (12 oz) caster sugar   ½ cinnamon stick
Pared zest and juice of 2 lemons   1 vanilla pod

Whichever syrup you are making, bring all the ingredients to the simmer, stirring to dissolve the sugar, then remove from the heat and allow to cool and infuse.

If you prefer a thicker, sweeter syrup, add an extra 100 g (4 oz) of caster sugar. If you are making the fruit stock syrup, it's best to leave the syrup with all ingredients included until needed, and then just drain off.

Stocks, Sauces and Basic Recipes

This chapter will give you all the basics you need for your stock and sauce making – plus a little more. Making stocks is a time-consuming occupation, but the results are worth every minute. A good stock can have the clarity of a consommé and when reduced, the shine will get even deeper and the taste even better.

ABOVE *Preparing Salsa Dressing (see p.243).*
LEFT *A selection of ingredients needed to make the dressings.*

If you don't have time to make your own stocks, I've included some alternatives that are available from most supermarkets – all of them have been tried and tested.

There are also some extras here that I picked up on my travels around Britain, such as the Irish Soda Bread.

In this section I have included some miscellaneous dishes. These are recipes that don't really need to be mixed with any particular dish in the rest of the book but are really good to eat so I decided to include them. There's the home-made Worcestershire sauce, lovely sprinkled on a steak or used to lift a sauce, Bone Marrow Dumplings, a great addition to any stew or soup, and my favourite Peanut Sauce, which reminds me of when I lived in Amsterdam years ago and was always eating chicken saté sticks with a hot peanut sauce to dip them in. The flavour is hot and spicy, so at your next barbecue have a go!

Fish Stock

To make a good fish stock, you'll need a friendly fishmonger. Turbot and sole bones produce the best stock, giving a good, full taste and clear jelly-like finish. The stock is good for poaching fish and for making fish soups and sauces. (For information on ready-made alternatives, see p.226).

MAKES about 2 litres (3½ pints)

1 large onion, sliced	1 bay leaf
1 leek, sliced	6 black peppercorns
2 celery sticks, sliced	900 g (2 lb) turbot or sole bones, washed
50 g (2 oz) unsalted butter	300 ml (10 fl oz) dry white wine
A few fresh parsley stalks	2.25 litres (4 pints) water

Sweat the vegetables in the butter without colouring. Add the parsley stalks, bay leaf and peppercorns. Chop the fish bones, making sure there are no blood clots left on them. Add them to the vegetables and continue to cook for a few minutes. Add the wine and boil to reduce until almost dry. Add the water and bring to a simmer. Allow to simmer for 20 minutes, then strain through a sieve. The stock is now ready to use, or to store for a few days in the fridge.

Chicken Stock

Chicken stock is one of our most important bases. It's used for most soups and many cream sauces. It's also very simple to make. I'm sure your local butcher will help you out with some chicken bones. If not, then cook a boiling fowl with vegetables in water and you will have a tasty stock and the bird to eat as well. You'll need a large stock pot, about 8.5 litre (15 pint) capacity, but if you don't have one you can easily reduce the quantities. (For information on ready-made alternatives see p.226).

MAKES 2.25 litres (4 pints)

2 onions, chopped	1 bay leaf
2 celery sticks, chopped	1 sprig of fresh thyme
2 leeks, chopped	A few black peppercorns
25 g (1 oz) unsalted butter	1.8 kg (4 lb) chicken carcasses, chopped
1 garlic clove, crushed	3.4 litres (6 pints) water

In a large stock pot, lightly soften the vegetables in the butter without colouring. Add the garlic, bay leaf, thyme, peppercorns and chopped carcasses. Cover with the cold water and bring to the simmer, skimming all the time. Allow the stock to simmer for 2–3 hours. Strain through a sieve. The stock is now ready to use and will keep well chilled or frozen.

Vegetable Stock

A very similar recipe for vegetable stock is included in the original Rhodes Around Britain *book. This recipe gives a different result. I have increased the quantity of carrots to give a sweeter taste to the stock. It can also be cooked to various stages leaving it at almost full capacity for risottos or vegetable stews, or reducing while cooking for butter sauces.*

MAKES about 900 ml (1½ pints)

350 g (12 oz) carrots
4 celery sticks
1 large onion
1 leek
25 g (1 oz) unsalted butter

1 bay leaf
1 sprig of fresh thyme
1.2 litres (2 pints) water
Salt and freshly ground black pepper

Roughly chop all the vegetables into 1 cm (½ in) dice. Melt the butter in a pan and add the vegetables. Cook on a low heat with the bay leaf and thyme for 10–12 minutes until softening. Add the water and bring to the simmer. Continue to simmer for about 20–30 minutes until the stock has reduced to about 900 ml (1½ pints). Strain through a sieve. The stock is now ready to use or can be stored for a few days in the fridge.

Veal or Beef Stock or *Jus*

This stock is a base to a lot of cooking, and really holds the essence of a good dish. Reading this recipe may well make you want to think twice about it, but it is worth making and so satisfying once made. It will give you great sauces and, of course, will store well in your freezer, so go on – have a go! It is best started in the morning which will allow the stock to cook throughout the day. Ask your butcher for a few beef or veal trimmings to make the stock.

If this really is too much, then a lot of good gravy bases can be found but do use them carefully, not making them too thick and strong. (For information on ready-made alternatives see p.226).

MAKES about 5 litres (9 pints) stock or 900 ml (1½ pints) *jus*

3 onions, halved	1 leek, chopped
2-3 tablespoons water	3-4 tomatoes, chopped
2.25 kg (5 lb) veal or beef bones	1 garlic clove, halved
225 g (8 oz) veal or beef trimmings	1 bay leaf
225 g (8 oz) carrots, coarsely chopped	1 sprig of fresh thyme
3 celery sticks, coarsely chopped	

Pre-heat the oven to 110°C/225°F/gas ½.

Lay the onion halves flat in a roasting tray with the water. Place in the very cool oven and allow to caramelize slowly until they have totally softened and coloured. This process will take 1–2 hours. The sugars in the onions will slowly cook and give a wonderful taste. Put the onions on one side.

Increase the oven temperature to 200°C/400°F/gas 6. Place all the bones and trimmings in a roasting tray and roast for about 30 minutes until well coloured. Roast the chopped carrots and celery in another roasting tray for about 20 minutes until lightly coloured.

When ready, add the bones, trimmings and vegetables to the onions in the pot along with the leeks, tomatoes, garlic, bay leaf and thyme. Fill the pot with cold water – you'll need about 5 litres (9 pints). Bring the stock to the simmer and skim off any impurities. Allow to cook for 6–8 hours, and with this you will achieve the maximum taste.

When ready, drain and discard the bones and vegetables. This is now your veal stock and you can cool it and freeze it in convenient quantities.

Alternatively, you can make a *jus* from the stock. Allow the liquid to boil and reduce down to about 900 ml (1½ pints), skimming occasionally. The stock should be thick and of a sauce consistency. Make sure that you taste all the time during reduction. If the sauce tastes right but is not thick enough, thicken it lightly with cornflour mixed in water. (Of course, I do hope that won't be necessary!) You now have a veal *jus*, a classic sauce.

Onion Gravy

Serve this classic gravy to accompany sauces or liver dishes.

SERVES 4

8 onions, thinly sliced
2 tablespoons water

600 ml (1 pint) Veal *Jus* (see p.224) or
bought alternative (see p.226)

Place the onions in a pan with the water and cook very slowly, stirring all the time. The sugar from the onions will slowly caramelize and become dark golden brown and sweet-tasting. The process will take about 2 hours. Add the veal *jus* and simmer for a further 30 minutes. The gravy will be even richer in taste and colour with a lovely, shiny finish.

Alternative Stocks and Sauces

Making fresh stocks at home is not always possible, so I've been out doing some homework on stocks and sauces in search of some good commercial alternatives to make the cooking of some of my dishes a little easier.

Fish and Chicken Stocks

Alternatives to these can be found in the chill cabinet of most Sainsbury's and other quality supermarkets. They are sold in plastic tubs each containing about 284 ml (about 9-10 fl oz). The beauty of these is they taste great, they have good colour and jelly texture, and they are sold as stocks ready to use. They really are the best I've found, but if you can't get hold of them there are also some good quality stock cubes.

Beef and Veal *Jus*

In the basic recipe, these start out as stocks and then for use in other recipes they are reduced to a sauce consistency. I've found a sauce which will cut out all of this, and is an instant *jus* to use as a base sauce in many of the recipes asking for veal or beef *jus*. Madeira Wine Gravy or White Wine Gravy are both made by Crosse & Blackwell in their Bonne Cuisine range, and should be available in just about every supermarket or good grocery shop. The Madeira flavour gives it good body and, when made, it has a lovely glossy finish. My only advice is to mix it with 600 ml (1 pint) of water instead of 300 ml (10 fl oz). This way, when slow-braising or stewing, there's room for reduction and it won't become too thick.

Other Sauces and Ingredients

Another sauce which I found very good is in the same range as the Madeira Wine Gravy: the hollandaise sauce. If you are unsure about making hollandaise, give this bought version a try; it's so easy.

There's only one other small suggestion. If you don't have any chillies, use the chilli sauce made by Maggi. It's sold in bottles and can be added slowly to taste.

As for dried pastas and ready-made pastry, all varieties can easily be found in local shops. If you're lucky enough to have a good delicatessen nearby, then perhaps buy your pasta there; it's often made on the premises.

I hope these few suggestions will help. It's always good to have a go at making your own stocks, sauces, jus and pasta, but cooking has to be practical and for regular use the products mentioned above will help tremendously. I certainly think they will make life for you an awful lot easier.

Tasting is an essential part of preparing any dish.

Vegetable Butter Sauce

This is a simple sauce which is easiest to make if you have an electric hand blender.

SERVES 4

150 ml (5 fl oz) reduced Vegetable Stock (see p.223)

50–75 g (2–3 oz) unsalted butter at room temperature

Salt and freshly ground white pepper

Pour the vegetable stock into a small pan and add 50 g (2 oz) of the butter. Bring to the simmer, whisking all the time. Season with salt and pepper. Whisk vigorously or use the hand blender and you should have a light creamy consistency. If the sauce seems a little too thin, then simply add the remaining butter and blend once more. The sauce is now ready.

Lemon Butter Sauce

This is one of the simplest possible sauces which has a silky texture and just enough to complement cod and salmon dishes in particular.

SERVES 4–6

225 g (8 oz) unsalted butter

Juice of 1 lemon

50 ml (2 fl oz) Chicken Stock (see p.222) or Vegetable Stock (see p.223)

Salt and freshly ground white pepper

Chop the butter into 1 cm (½ in) pieces and put it into a pan with the lemon juice and stock. Bring to a simmer, whisking all the time. Do not allow the sauce to boil or the butter will separate. If it is too thick, add more stock. If you like a sharper taste, add more lemon juice. Season with salt and pepper and serve immediately. To give a creamier texture, simply blitz the sauce with an electric hand blender.

Fennel Butter Sauce

This is a good sauce for fish. The aniseed flavour of fennel is helped by the addition of star anise in the cooking liquor. To increase the flavour for a fish dish, use some Fish Stock (see p.221) in the reduction for the sauce. However, you'll find that fennel creates a good stock and when reduced by three-quarters should be strong enough on its own.

SERVES 4

2 fennel bulbs	1–2 star anise
900 ml (1½ pints) water	Salt
Juice of 1 lemon	50-75 g (2–3 oz) unsalted butter

Trim the root and top stalks from the fennel. Place in boiling water with the lemon juice, star anise and a pinch of salt. Return to the boil, cover the fennel with a butter paper or greaseproof and simmer until tender; this will take about 20–30 minutes. When ready, a sharp knife will just be able to reach the centre of the bulb.

Remove the fennel bulbs, then boil and reduce the cooking liquor down to about 150-300 ml (5-10 fl oz) to give a good, strong taste. Dice the fennel into 5 mm (¼ in) pieces. The liquor can now be finished with the butter, just whisking it in to create a fennel butter sauce. Remove the star anise. Blitz the sauce with a hand blender to give a more creamy texture. Add the fennel and warm through. Check and adjust the seasoning.

Variations

Chopped chives, tarragon or mint could be added to this sauce at the last minute to give it another flavour.

Red Wine Sauce

This sauce tastes good with almost any meat – chicken, beef, pork, veal – and even eats well with baked fish.

MAKES about 1.2 litres (2 pints)

4 shallots, chopped
1 large carrot, chopped
2 celery sticks, chopped
25 g (1 oz) unsalted butter
1 garlic clove, crushed
1 bay leaf
1 sprig of fresh thyme

225 g (8 oz) beef skirt or beef trimmings
   (optional)
1 tablespoon olive oil (optional)
1 bottle red wine
1.2 litres (2 pints) Veal *Jus* (see p.224) or
   bought alternative (see p.226)
Salt and freshly ground white pepper

In a large pan, cook the chopped vegetables in a little butter with the garlic and herbs, allowing them to colour. In a frying-pan, fry the meat, if used, in the oil, colouring on all sides, then add the meat to the vegetables. Pour the red wine into the frying-pan to release any flavours from the trimmings. Scrape and stir, then pour the wine on to the meat and vegetables and boil to reduce until almost dry.

Add the veal *jus* and bring to the simmer, skim off any impurities, then simmer the sauce gently for 30 minutes. Pass through a sieve, squeezing all the juices from the vegetables and meat. Check for seasoning and you now have a rich, glistening red wine sauce.

Quick Red Wine Sauce

At work I always make fresh stocks, gravies and sauces, but when you're at home it's not often or ever possible. But there is always an alternative. Whenever making packet sauces it's best to add half again or even double the quantity of water given in the recipe to give a better consistency. Bonne Cuisine Madeira Wine Gravy is a good one to use. To make the sauce even simpler, you can leave out the shallots, bay leaf and peppercorns.

MAKES about 1.2 litres (2 pints)

600 ml (1 pint) red wine
2 shallots, sliced
1 bay leaf

A few black peppercorns
1 packet instant gravy made up with
900 ml (1½ pints) water

To make this red wine sauce, bring the wine to the boil with the shallots, bay leaf and peppercorns, then boil until reduced by three-quarters, leaving about 150 ml (5 fl oz) of strong red wine. Add the gravy and cook for a few minutes. Strain before serving.

Tomato Coulis

This is a very useful basic for all sorts of recipes.

MAKES about 900 ml (1½ pints)

1 large onion, chopped
2 celery sticks, chopped
1 large carrot, chopped
1 garlic clove, crushed
A few fresh basil or tarragon leaves or a
    pinch of dried tarragon
1 sprig of fresh thyme or a pinch of
    dried thyme
2 tablespoons olive oil

50 g (2 oz) unsalted butter
150 ml (5 fl oz) dry white wine
450 g (1 lb) tomatoes, chopped
300 ml (10 fl oz) Chicken Stock (see
    p.222) or Vegetable Stock (see p.223)
1 tablespoon tomato purée
Salt and freshly ground white pepper
A few drops of Spicing Essence (see
    p.233) (optional)

Cook the chopped onion, celery and carrot with the garlic and herbs in the olive oil and butter for a few minutes until softened. Add the white wine and boil to reduce until almost dry. Add the tomatoes and cook for a few minutes, then add the stock and tomato purée, bring to the simmer, cover with a lid and continue to cook for 20 minutes. Liquidize the sauce, then push it through a sieve to give a smooth sauce consistency. If the sauce is a little thick, add more stock to reach the right consistency. Season to taste with salt and pepper. The coulis is now ready. To make the sauce more spicy, add a few drops of spicing essence at a time, if using, whisking and tasting until you have the flavour you want.

Variations

You can also use this recipe to make a red pepper coulis. Just replace 350 g (12 oz) of the tomatoes with an equal weight of seeded red peppers, then follow the same procedure.

Spicing Essence

I think this little trick comes from Escoffier's days; it is often used for spicing up a sauce or other dish. It was also occasionally used to mask the flavours of a meat that wasn't quite right! Well, I'm glad to say that I use it purely for enhancing flavours, and it works its magic particularly with Tomato Coulis (see p.232).

MAKES about 150 ml (5 fl oz)

50 g (2 oz) demerara sugar   150 ml (5 fl oz) malt vinegar

Simply dissolve the sugar in the vinegar, then boil for a few minutes until reduced to a syrup. It is now ready to use, and only a few drops are needed to spice your sauces. After that, it can be kept in an airtight jar in the fridge for as long as you like.

Tomato Dressing or Sauce

This tomato dressing can also be a thick fresh tomato sauce. When tomatoes are cooking, they create a lot of excess water. This sauce is cooked until almost all the water has evaporated, leaving you with almost a fresh tomato purée. To make the sauce into a dressing, loosen with Basic Vinaigrette (see p.241) or olive oil to taste.

SERVES 4

15 g (½ oz) unsalted butter
1 tablespoon olive oil
½ onion, finely chopped
1 small garlic clove, crushed
1 glass white wine

450 g (1 lb) ripe tomatoes, skinned and
     seeded
1 teaspoon tomato purée
Salt and freshly ground black pepper

Melt the butter with the olive oil in a warm pan until the butter begins to bubble. Add the onion and garlic and cook for a few minutes until the onions have softened. Pour the white wine over the onions and bring to the boil. Continue to boil until the wine has reduced and is almost dry.

While this is reducing, chop the tomatoes to a coarse pulp. Add the tomatoes and tomato purée to the pan and bring to the simmer. While the tomatoes are cooking, a lot of water will be created, so allow this to evaporate. Season with salt and pepper and the sauce is ready.

Spicy Tomato Sauce

This sauce goes so well with seafood of all types. It's almost like eating a loose, spicy tomato chutney. Once made, it can be kept chilled for up to two weeks.

MAKES about 450 g (1 lb)

85 ml (3 fl oz) olive oil
3 shallots or 2 onions, finely chopped
2 garlic cloves, crushed
A few fresh basil, thyme and tarragon leaves
900 g (2 lb) tomatoes, skinned and seeded

2 tablespoons red wine vinegar
1 teaspoon caster sugar
Salt
2–3 drops of Tabasco sauce

Warm the olive oil in a pan and add the chopped shallots or onions, the garlic and herbs. It's best to have the herbs in sprigs as these can then be easily removed at the end of cooking. Allow the shallots and herbs to cook gently for 4–5 minutes until tender.

Cut the tomato flesh into 5 mm (¼ in) dice and add to the shallots. Have the pan on a very low heat, just on a light simmer, and cook for about 45 minutes. The sauce may cook a little quicker or take a little longer – this will really depend on the water content of the tomatoes. After 45 minutes, add the wine vinegar and sugar and cook for a further 15 minutes. The tomatoes should have taken on an almost lumpy sauce texture; if the sauce is very thick, simply fold in a little more olive oil. Allow to cool until just warm, then season with salt and Tabasco.

Pesto Sauce

Pesto sauce can be bought in most supermarkets and food stores, but here is a simple version to make yourself. No Parmesan will be needed for this sauce.

SERVES 4

50 g (2 oz) pinenuts
150 ml (5 fl oz) olive oil
1 small garlic clove

1 large bunch of basil
Salt and freshly ground black pepper

Simply colour the nuts lightly in the olive oil, then allow to cool. Add the crushed garlic clove, basil, a pinch of salt and pepper and blend to a purée. This is now ready and can be kept for 2–3 days in the fridge.

Hollandaise Sauce

This is a quick way of making a French classic.

MAKES about 250 ml (8 fl oz)

225 g (8 oz) unsalted butter
2 egg yolks
1 tablespoon warm water

Juice of ½ lemon
Salt and cayenne pepper or freshly
  ground white pepper

Melt the butter in a pan, then leave it to cool slightly so that it is just warm when added to the sauce; if it is too hot, the sauce will curdle. The butter will have separated, so you will only be adding the butter oil to the sauce. This is clarified butter.

Add the egg yolks to the water in a bowl and whisk over a pan of hot water until cooked and thickened. Remove from the heat and add the clarified butter, whisking until the sauce is thick. Add the lemon juice and season with salt and cayenne or white pepper.

Worcestershire Sauce

I enjoy finding, trying and hopefully developing recipes like this. I looked through a lot of old cookery books to find this so that I could have a go at matching the famous bottle we all know and use. Well, it's not quite the same, and you can't really match that distinctive taste, but it's fun and interesting to make, especially when you have to wait a few weeks for the result!

The Worcestershire sauce recipe must be 160 years old. The recipe was found and given to the makers in India. They soon discovered how popular the sauce was and I don't think they ever looked back.

MAKES 900 ml (1½ pints)

600 ml (1 pint) malt vinegar
150 ml (5 fl oz) walnut or mushroom
   ketchup
2 tablespoons anchovy essence
2 shallots or 1 onion, finely chopped
3 tablespoons soy sauce

A pinch of cayenne
A pinch of ground cinnamon
1 garlic clove, crushed
A pinch of freshly grated nutmeg
A pinch of ground cardamom
A pinch of salt

There are a few ways of putting this recipe together.

The first is simply to mix all the ingredients and keep in an airtight bottle or container for 2–3 weeks, making sure the bottle is shaken every day.

Another way is to mix all the liquid ingredients with the onion and garlic, bring to the boil and simmer for 30 minutes before adding the spices and salt. Bottle and cool, make airtight and keep for two weeks, shaking every day.

The mix can also be made without the herbs, just mixing the liquids and onion. This will still need to be left and shaken every day for 2–3 weeks.

After the marinating period, strain the sauce before use.

Peanut Sauce

This is the sauce that you find in Thai restaurants served with chicken or pork satay. It's a good sauce to go with barbecued chicken pieces or wings, such as my recipe on page 51. You can follow the recipe with lemon and paprika, marinate simply in lime juice, or just plain grill the chicken. You can lift the flavours in the peanut sauce with a dash of lime juice, too.

SERVES 4

225 g (8 oz) crunchy peanut butter
3 garlic cloves, crushed
15 fresh coriander leaves
50 ml (2 fl oz) soy sauce

2 tablespoons Japanese sake
¼–½ teaspoon chilli oil
120 ml (4 fl oz) coconut milk
Water

In a food processor, blend the peanut butter with the garlic and coriander. In a separate jug, mix the soy sauce, sake, chilli oil and coconut milk. With the motor running, pour the mixture slowly into the processor until all the liquid has blended in. The sauce should be thick but not set like peanut butter. If the sauce is too thick, just loosen it by adding a tablespoon of water at a time. The sauce can be served warmed or kept chilled for 2–3 days.

Cranberry *Jus* or Gravy

The flavour of this sauce can be helped by taking a good handful of vegetable mirepoix *(roughly chopped carrots, shallots or onions, celery and leeks) and cooking them with 2 bay leaves and a sprig of fresh thyme for a few minutes before adding the red wine. The sauce will then need to be sieved before adding the cranberry sauce.*

SERVES 4–8

2 glasses red wine
600 ml (1 pint) Veal *Jus* (see p.224) or
　alternative (see p.226)

2 large tablespoons Cranberry Sauce
　(see p.239)

Boil the red wine until reduced by two-thirds. Add the veal *jus* or alternative and bring the sauce to the simmer. Add the cranberry sauce and continue to simmer gently for 10–15 minutes. Stir in the cranberry sauce until well blended.

Variations

To make a quick cranberry-flavoured sauce just take 600 ml (1 pint) of *jus* alternative (see p.226) and add 2 tablespoons of bought or home-made cranberry jelly. More can be added to adjust the taste to your liking.

Cranberry Sauce with Orange

The obvious main ingredient here is, of course, the cranberries. Cranberry sauce can be made with just cranberries, sugar and a little water, but I replace the water with orange juice, and spice it with a little port; a combination that has become a classic. I also like to add a little chopped shallot to help the savoury taste of the dish.

This sauce eats very well with roast turkey, pork or game and with any of the bubble and squeak variations. It's also good to serve with cold meats and pies.

SERVES 4

450 g (1 lb) fresh cranberries
100 g (4 oz) caster sugar
Juice of 2 large oranges

½ teaspoon very finely chopped shallots
1 glass of port

Simply place all the ingredients in a pan and bring to a simmer. Cook gently for 10–15 minutes until the cranberries are just beginning to break.

Vinegars and Oils

Malt vinegar is probably the best known, especially for sprinkling on your fish and chips! Malt vinegar is made from malted barley (as, of course, is whisky!), and gets its colour from caramel. The strongest of vinegars, it is used mostly for pickling, and I've often used it in chutney recipes where it helps to achieve the right acidity for the ingredients. Don't use it in basic dressings as its strength is just too much for salads.

Red and white wine vinegars are the ones to use for most general dressings and purposes. Red wine vinegar is the best. Wine vinegars are allowed to mature slowly in barrels until the vinegars have turned the alcohol into acetic acid. They can be made more swiftly by heating, but this tends to destroy some of the flavours.

Balsamic vinegar must be the most-used vinegar in modern cookery, which doesn't surprise me as it really is astounding. There are many cheap copies on the market which aren't worth buying. Real balsamic vinegar is made from Trebbiano grapes and should be a minimum of five years old to have any true flavour. The older it gets, the better and stronger it tastes but, of course, the more expensive it is to buy. Twelve-year-old balsamic is a great medium and although it's pricey, you need very little because of its immense flavour. Some balsamics can be as old as forty years, but this is very rare and you'll probably have to wait another forty years to try one!

Oils

The oils that I generally use are extra-virgin olive oil and ground-nut (peanut) oil.

*Ground-nut is a very basic oil which is used in France (*huile à l'arachide*) as a base in most dressings and in frying. It's very similar to sunflower oil and has quite a bland flavour. In basic dressings I mix it with olive oil, which prevents the dressing from becoming too overpowering. It is also cheaper to make and works well on all simple salads.*

Virgin olive oil is an oil from the first pressing which is totally pure, without any heating or chemical processing. The 'extra' in front applies to its low acidity grade. Extra-virgin oil has 1 per cent acidity, which is the lowest and the best.

Basic Vinaigrette

This basic recipe is very convenient. Once made, it can sit in your fridge and be used at any time and for any dish you might fancy. The vinegar just gives a very slight sweetness to the taste.

MAKES 600 ml (1 pint)

300 ml (10 fl oz) extra-virgin olive oil (French or Italian)	3–4 sprigs of fresh thyme
300 ml (10 fl oz) ground-nut oil	12 black peppercorns, lightly crushed
25 ml (1 fl oz) balsamic vinegar	3 shallots, finely chopped
1 bunch of fresh basil	2 garlic cloves, crushed
½ bunch of fresh tarragon	1 bay leaf
	1 teaspoon coarse sea salt

Warm the olive and ground-nut oils together. Place all the remaining ingredients into a 750 ml (1¼ pint) bottle. Pour the oil into the bottle and close with a cork or screw top. For the best results, leave to marinate for a week, which will allow the flavours to enhance the oils. To help the dressing along, shake the bottle once a day. Taste for seasoning before use.

Red Wine Vinaigrette

This is a basic recipe to which you can add your favourite herbs. The best to use, unchopped, are basil, tarragon or thyme. When you are going to use the dressing just add some chopped fresh chives, basil, thyme or tarragon to finish the dressing.

MAKES about 600 ml (1 pint)

4 shallots or 1 large onion, finely
    chopped
2 garlic cloves, crushed
300 ml (10 fl oz) red wine

300 ml (10 fl oz) red wine vinegar
2 teaspoons Dijon mustard
600 ml (1 pint) olive oil
Salt and freshly ground black pepper

Mix the shallots or onion with the garlic in a pan and add the red wine. Bring to the boil, then boil to reduce until almost dry. Add the red wine vinegar and boil to reduce by three-quarters. Remove the pan from the heat.

While the shallots are still warm, add the Dijon mustard and blend in with the olive oil. Season with salt and pepper. The dressing can now be left to cool and then bottled. Chilled, it keeps for several weeks.

Mayonnaise

Home-made mayonnaise is so much tastier than bought mayonnaise. Use it with potatoes in a salad, or as a dressing for sandwiches.

MAKES about 600 ml (1 pint)

3 egg yolks
1 tablespoon malt, white wine or
    balsamic vinegar
A pinch of English or Dijon mustard

Salt and freshly ground white pepper
300 ml (10 fl oz) olive oil
1 teaspoon hot water
A few drops of lemon juice (optional)

Whisk the egg yolks, vinegar, mustard and seasonings together, then slowly add the olive oil, whisking continuously. When all the oil has been added, finish with the hot water and correct the seasoning. A few drops of lemon juice can be added to enhance the taste.

Vierge Dressing

This dressing has a very different flavour and lends itself best to fish dishes. I was first inspired to make it whilst staying at La Côte St Jacques in Joigny, France, in the mid 1980s when it was served with a red mullet dish. That restaurant now has three Michelin stars.

MAKES 600 ml (1 pint)

600 ml (1 pint) extra-virgin olive oil (French or Italian)
15 g (½ oz) coriander seeds, crushed
1 bunch of fresh tarragon

12 black peppercorns, crushed
4 shallots, chopped
2 garlic cloves, crushed
A pinch of sea salt

Warm the olive oil with the coriander seeds. Place the remaining ingredients in a 600 ml (1 pint) screw-top jar and pour the oil and coriander on top. Screw on the lid and leave to marinate for 1 week, shaking the bottle daily.

Salsa Dressing

Salsa is a Mexican relish that has so many variations. It's really a fresh sweet and sour chutney, come sauce, come dressing. Another ingredient is chillies, so not only is it sweet and sour but hot, too! This recipe goes well with hot or cold fish, meats, chicken or you can even use it as a relish for a hamburger. The most classic version is Salsa Verde, a green chutney with garlic, parsley, mint, mustard, capers, green chillies, oil and vinegar. There are also red salsas and fruit salsas and more, but this we'll just call 'Salsa Dressing'!

SERVES 4

2 red onions, finely chopped
2 green peppers, seeded and diced
2 green chillies, seeded and finely diced
1 garlic clove, finely chopped
1 tablespoon olive oil

Juice of 1–2 limes
8 plum or salad tomatoes, skinned, seeded and diced
Salt

Mix together the diced red onions, green peppers, chillies and garlic. Add the olive oil and the juice of 1 lime. Add the tomato flesh and stir in well to slightly break down the tomato flesh. Adjust the seasoning with a good pinch of salt.

The salsa should have a good balance of flavours. More lime juice maybe needed to lift the other tastes. The salsa is now ready and can be kept in the fridge for a few days.

Cucumber Pickle

This pickle goes very well with salads. It can be served with pork pies, corned beef or just with cold meats. But I like to serve it with fish, in particular salmon. We've all heard of smoked salmon and cucumber sandwiches, a classic combination. This pickle eats very well with simple poached salmon, but I particularly like it with Seared Peppered Salmon (p.32).

Serves 4

4 cucumbers, peeled and de-seeded
1½ teaspoons salt
150 ml (5 fl oz) ground-nut oil
1 teaspoon chilli oil
1 large garlic clove, crushed

1 fresh red chilli, finely chopped
2 tablespoons soy sauce
25 g (1 oz) caster sugar
2 tablespoons white wine vinegar
½ bunch of spring onions, thinly sliced

Grate the cucumbers on a basic cheese grater. Mix the salt with the cucumber, place in a colander and allow to drain for 20 minutes. This will take out any excess water.

Warm the ground-nut and chilli oils with the crushed garlic and finely chopped red chilli for a few minutes. Add the soy sauce, sugar and white wine vinegar and bring to the simmer. Lightly dry off the cucumber. Mix the spring onions with the cucumber, then add the mixture to the simmering oil and increase the heat, stirring for 30 seconds. Remove from the heat and tip the pickle on to a deep tray or into a large cold saucepan to cool as quickly as possible. Place in an airtight jar.

Bone Marrow Dumplings

These dumplings can be eaten as a savoury dish and go particularly well with pan-fried diced bacon, button onions and button mushrooms in a red wine sauce. They are used mostly as an accompaniment in beef stews and casseroles but I also use them with a grilled steak in red wine sauce. Just one good dumpling a portion is enough, and the beauty of using this recipe is that it keeps for three or four days if chilled. So if you want to lift just a simple, ordinary steak then have a go at this recipe.

Serves 4

100 g (4 oz) fresh bone marrow
100 g (4 oz) white breadcrumbs
2 tablespoons double cream
3–4 egg yolks
1 heaped tablespoon chopped fresh
    parsley

A pinch of freshly grated nutmeg
Salt and freshly ground black pepper
Chicken Stock (see p.222) or water

Break the bone marrow down in a food processor, then add the breadcrumbs. Add the cream and 3 yolks with the chopped parsley. Add the remaining yolk if necessary to make a stiff mixture. Season with nutmeg, salt and pepper and chill for 1 hour before cooking to help set the mix.

Bring a pan of stock or water to the boil. The mix can be either shaped into ovals between 2 tablespoons or simply rolled into balls and dropped into simmering stock. The dumplings should be ready in 10–15 minutes. You can then add them to a stew or braised dish.

Variations

Try using other herbs instead of the parsley; thyme or sage taste particularly good.

Soda Bread

This is a recipe I tried in Ireland – another easy recipe with great results. The first time I ate soda bread, it was filled with bacon and fried egg with a big mug of tea for breakfast – it was lovely. So if you want to have a go at making your own bread for your next 'full Irish / English', follow this recipe.

If you can find traditional Irish self-raising soda bread flour, all you need to add is the salt and buttermilk, but this recipe will work just as well.

Serves 4

350 g (12 oz) plain flour
1 level tablespoon bicarbonate of soda

A good pinch of salt
300 ml (10 fl oz) buttermilk

Pre-heat the oven to 190°C/375°F/gas 5.

Sift the flour, bicarbonate of soda and salt together and make a well in the centre. Pour in the buttermilk and mix gently to form a dough. Knead until smooth without overworking. Lightly dust the work surface with flour and roll out the dough to a circle about 2 cm (¾ in) thick. Cut the circle into quarters. Place on a baking sheet and bake in the pre-heated oven for 30–40 minutes until golden brown and hollow-sounding when tapped.

To cool and keep crispy, stand the bread on a wire rack. If you prefer a softer bread, wrap in a cloth to cool.

Variations

You can cook the bread on a griddle or frying-pan. Heat the pan over a moderate heat. To test the temperature, sprinkle a little flour on the pan; it should turn slightly off-white. Sit the bread into the pan and cook for 12–15 minutes on each side.

Soda Bread.

Beremeal Bannocks

Another recipe from my Scottish friend, this traditionally uses beremeal, which is an ancient northern barley. If you can't get hold of it, use oatmeal or wholemeal flour. I had a go at making these while staying in Scotland. They are easy and fun to make and eat superbly.

SERVES 4–6

100 g (4 oz) plain flour
1 teaspoon salt
2 heaped teaspoons bicarbonate of soda
1 heaped teaspoon cream of tartar

350 g (12 oz) beremeal or oatmeal
50 g (2 oz) unsalted butter
300–600 ml (½–1 pint) buttermilk

Sift the flour with the salt, bicarbonate of soda and cream of tartar. Add the beremeal or oatmeal. Rub in the butter, then gradually add the buttermilk, mixing to form a soft dough. You may not need all the buttermilk; it will depend on the meal you are using.

Warm a frying-pan or griddle. Shape the mix with a rolling pin or push and shape it by hand into a circle 3 cm (1¼ in) deep; or you might find it easier to shape it into smaller loaves. Cook the bannocks directly on the griddle or in the pan over a medium heat for 2–3 minutes each side. Serve at once.

Pasta Dough

This pasta dough can be used for lasagne, fettucine, ravioli and many more pasta dishes. You can make it by hand or in a food processor. It also freezes very well.

MAKES 450 g (1 lb) to SERVE 4

250 g (9 oz) fine semolina or plain flour
A pinch of salt
½ teaspoon olive oil

2 eggs
3 egg yolks

Mix the semolina or flour with the salt and olive oil and mix well for 1 minute. Add the eggs and egg yolks and stir well until it becomes a dough. Knead the dough for 1–3 minutes until it has a smooth texture. Wrap it in cling film and chill for 30 minutes to rest.

The pasta is now ready to use. It can be rolled, cut and cooked straight away, or cut and left to dry and used later. If dried, the pasta will always take a little longer to cook.

More Ideas

I hope this book has given you lots of ideas and alternatives to a range of quite basic recipes. I could probably go on and on throwing ideas at you, hoping that you'll all have a go at at least one, but I have to stop somewhere. Just before I finish, though, I've got a few more for you to have a look at and think about.

Potted Salmon (see p.24) can quite easily be changed to potted shrimps. Just cook the butter with the shallots and herbs, then remove from the heat and add peeled shrimps or prawns and spoon into the moulds.

Banana Ice-cream (see p.192) can be really lifted by adding 2 tablespoons of natural yoghurt and 3 tablespoons of toffee (page 164). A brilliant ice-cream.

The crispy shrimp used in a skate dish (see p.76) can be used in a warm salad with lots of crunchy shrimps sprinkled over the top.

The lager batter (see p.72) can be used to deep-fry almost anything: vegetables, meat balls, sausage, fish.

Try a good Barnsley lamb chop (double chop) grilled with Hollandaise Sauce (see p.235) flavoured with chopped mint and served with home-made crisps (see p.22).

Calves' liver, cut into 2.5 cm (1 in) slices, can be grilled to medium, then sliced and served with Champ (see p.134) or Dijon Mustard Mashed Potatoes (see p.91).

All the herbs I use in the book are fresh. If you can't get them, then use dried herbs tied in muslin cloth or buy the tea-bag bouquet garni.

The potatoes used in the cod dish (see p.68) can be turned into a complete starter. Just mix them with slices of red and green peppers lightly cooked in olive oil with garlic, basil, tarragon and tomatoes. Sit a warm poached egg on top of each portion and your starter is ready.

Another good duck breast dish is to score and grill the breast, keeping the skin crispy, and serve it with home-made chips and a maltaise sauce. This is Hollandaise Sauce (see p.235) with a reduced blood orange juice. Straight orange juice can be used, reducing down until very strong. Add it to the hollandaise and you have an orange sauce. Serve this with the duck breast and you have a modern canard à l'orange.

Parsnips are so versatile. Once you've tried them roasted or puréed, try frying cooked parsnips in batter, like the beetroot on page 138

Here's one of my favourite alternatives. If you're making one of the risottos and have some left over, spread it into a dish or tray 2.5 cm (1 in) deep and allow it to set in the fridge. Once set, the risotto can be cut out with round pastry cutters (like fish cakes) or rolled into balls and dusted with flour. There are now several ways of cooking them:

shallow-fry in butter until golden brown;

roll in egg and breadcrumbs and deep-fry until golden;

dip in savoury pancake mix and shallow-fry until golden on both sides.

Any of these methods will give you golden risotto cakes with creamy risotto inside. These eat well as a separate starter, with a fish or meat main course or even small ones made as canapés.

A good alternative for the Mushroom Risotto (see p.57) is to turn it into a breakfast risotto. Crispy pieces of bacon can be added or sprinkled over the black pudding and then a poached or fried egg placed on top.

Here's an extra idea for the duck breast dish on page 86: just replace the parsnip with neeps and tatties.

So that's it, I've had to stop. My whole feeling about cooking is never to be afraid of any dish or ingredient. If you believe in it, then try it.

Until the next time ...

Index

Page numbers in *italic* refer to the illustrations